KITCHEN BLUES

Rabbi Lionel Blue was born and brought up in the East End of London. He studied History at Balliol, Judaism in the Leo Baeck College where he now lectures in Comparative Religion, mysticism in Christian priories and at the feet of Hindu gurus, and Life everywhere.

He has been a Rabbi in London, and was 'the bishop of a bankrupt diocese' in post holocaust Europe. To his own surprise he is now a pillar of the religious establishment in charge of the Ecclesiastical Court of the Reform Synagogues of Great Britain.

He broadcasts frequently on television and radio with regular contributions to BBC Radio 4's 'Thought for the Day' and, as a guest cook, to *Pebble Mill at One*. He is cookery editor for *The Universe* and writes a regular column for the *London Standard*. He is the author of several books including *To Heaven with Scribes and Pharisees* (explaining Judaism to Christians) and *A Backdoor to Heaven* (explaining his own religion to himself). A new book, *Bolts from the Blue*, will be published in Autumn 1986.

Rabbi Blue likes people, train journeys, markets and has religious experiences in hospital waiting rooms and on the Central line of London's Underground Railway.

KITCHEN BLUES

Recipes for Body and Soul

RABBI LIONEL BLUE

LONDON
VICTOR GOLLANCZ LTD
1986

First published in Great Britain 1985
by Victor Gollancz Ltd,
14 Henrietta Street, London WC2E 8QJ

First published in Gollancz Paperbacks 1986

British Library Cataloguing in Publication Data
Blue, Lionel
  Kitchen blues: recipes for body and soul.
  1. Cookery, Jewish
  I. Title
  641.5'676   TX724

  ISBN 0-575-03733-4
  ISBN 0-575-03898-5 pbk

Photoset in Great Britain by
Rowland Phototypesetting Ltd, Bury St Edmunds, Suffolk
Printed in Finland by Werner Söderström Oy

Kitchen talk

When I became a minister I was very zealous and determined to visit everybody. It was quite embarrassing for my congregation. I used to turn up just as a lady was putting her hair in curlers, or an officer of my synagogue was getting into his bath. They didn't know what to do with me, so they gave me a whisky and a chair in the parlour, and hoped (in whispers to each other) I would keep quiet and go.

It had never occurred to me that my consolations of religion were not always in demand. But as my congregation and I came to know each other, and sized each other up, I graduated from the parlour to the kitchen.

I loosened my tie, and propped my hands on the table, and they meandered about their kitchens in curlers and gardening clothes, finding bits for me to eat, because once again I was trying not to smoke. The profundities of life and cooking intermingled with the bitter-sweet jokes of Jewish life. We touched so many deep things in a light way, that I have never lost my respect for kitchen talk.

Later on I found this kind of conversation was not limited to Jews. The same kind of kitchen talk went on in the kitchens of Anglican rectories, Catholic priories, and the kitchen of *The Universe* office.

I learned a lot about religion in my universities and seminary. I learned religion, not about it, in listening to the life experience of ordinary people in kitchens.

Gossip

I recently read a learned work about the transmission of sacred texts. None of the scribes could ever leave anything alone. They all wanted to improve their texts. (They had the same urge as DIY enthusiasts or compulsive reformers.) The author doubted if this anonymous process of change was possible in our more self-conscious days. Well it is like that in cookery. Recipes are transformed through a chain of tradition. (The religious traditions have stiffened up and don't flow so easily these days.) I have never yet met anyone who cooked strictly according to the book, just as I have never met anyone who has lived that way either. Nor would I like to. Every person (and animal) is so special, and I enjoy human vagaries. I prefer my recipes and my friends to be free-range like my chicken.

In Jewish Law you are commanded to mention your teacher when you have learnt something of value. You are supposed to begin any wise statement with the phrase, 'I learned this in the name of my master, Rabbi So-and-so.' Therefore at the beginning of this book, I should like to mention the many mistresses of kitchens and a few masters, my kitchen sages, and culinary rabbis all.

Rowanne Pascoe, the sparkling editor of *The Universe* itself, whose tastes are truly catholic, embracing cooking, domestic cats and stray rabbis. Also Kieron, Gerry, Thea, and my other mates on that compulsive journal.

Isabelle in Paris who works like a carthorse and looks as fragile as a flower. She can even change plugs, which I still can't.

Eva like the White Rabbit is always late for the duchess's party because her lame ducks and stray lambs are too many and her time is too short.

Janny does not compromise. Her guests never wash up, she serves real butter and uses cloth napkins.

Clare, who keeps an open house, and a synagogue open.

Phyllis, my secretary, the provider of cake and kindness.

Pauline, a kindly artist, and a good Samaritan whose kitchen has been my refuge.

Daphne, in whose company sausages and claret are a delight.

Chani, a mystic and a flautist who pipes me towards vegetarian cooking.

Jacqueline who brings back the taste of my student days in Holland.

Judith whose kindness supported me in difficult times as her chocolate-roll supported her.

Elizabeth who surprises herself as she surprises others with her good cooking.

My mother and my aunt who typed and tasted and survived.

Kim who tried to teach me how to use a sextant and make a roux. For the former my apologies, for the latter my thanks.

Father Gordian and Sister Maura who have been accepted into the kitchen of Jewish life.

Jim who gave me a taste of the North and showed me that the jungle does not begin at Watford.

Jan and Krystyna whose recipes from Eastern Europe remind me of my childhood and my grandmother.

William who can deal with all the things I can't, such as wet rot, wallpaper and walnut cake.

Hugo, Willy and Ernest who make good things without fuss.

Tina and Guy who read through my manuscript, risking indigestion.

I have put my friend Rowanne at the head of the list because it was she who 'discovered' me. When Rowanne came to *The Universe* she asked me to fill in for the family page for a couple of weeks. Well I've been filling in now for years. I am a Rabbi who has wandered into a universal catholic family and become an odd part of it – rather like 'The Man who came to Dinner', someone who drops in for a snack, and stays to dinner, and then becomes the lodger. Much of the material will be familiar then to readers of that racy and readable journal. I can only say that come Fridays, when it arrives at my home, there is a tussle as to who gets it first, and as we are a Jewish household that is quite something.

I like its mixture of spiritual pep and pictures and gossip, and whenever I'm feeling low I turn to the adverts. They are so much more intimate, materially and spiritually, than the equivalent Jewish or Protestant ones.

L.B.
1985

Useful chat

I have a pair of scales but don't really have time to use them and my cooking isn't the type to need that accuracy. I do use a measuring cone which copes with my normal needs – flour, sugar, lentils, rice, American equivalents etc. When I can't find it, I use a teacup without a handle and a mug with bunnies on it. The former contains about the equivalent of an American cup and the latter about the equivalent of a British cup (8 fluid oz and 10 fluid oz respectively).

I also use the spoons in my kitchen drawer as measures (teaspoon, tablespoon, dessert spoon and coffee spoon). When I get round to organizing my kitchen (for I have just moved house), I am going to buy a set of American cup and spoon measures, and the same for metric. I shall make sure they are different colours so that I can't get them mixed up.

I have given the measures, weights and volumes in old-fashioned pounds, ounces and pints. These have been replaced by metric measurements, but for quite a while, both systems will be in use as well as the American, which is very convenient except for sticky things like butter, syrup and treacle. Some simple conversion advice is given at the beginning of the book.

I welcome such helps as slow cookers and microwaves, but only one machine has become really important and that is a food processor. I bought one years ago for about £30 and I've never regretted it. I often have to prepare a meal for guests after a busy day at the office. Yes: I could mince and purée and chop without it, but I wouldn't. I would just go to the nearest takeaway instead. So my machine has more than earned its keep.

Another idiosyncrasy. I have set out many recipes so that the measurements are easy to remember, as for example '666,333 Cake'. Such simple formulae become as automatic as driving or touch-typing. This causes fewer mistakes when you are trying to cook before you have laid to rest the tensions of the office, and you are on the simmer as well as your saucepan.

The recipes themselves are a various lot. Some I have eaten in gourmet restaurants and some I consumed with gusto sitting on a pavement in a slum. All of them have given me pleasure and that is why they are here. I didn't know whether to group these pieces gastronomically or spiritually. I decided on the former because it's easier to sort out confusions in the tummy, than the soul.

I have classified the recipes into groups – appetizers, soups, hearty eating and so on. But recipes, like life, escape all classification. A soup can be hearty eating, and what for Britons is a sweet, in America is a starter. I suggest a quick browse through the spiritual and culinary menus.

Because of the Jewish food laws, smoked meat such as beef or sausage is used in place of bacon or other pork products. Dairy products are not used with meat, so margarine or oil replaces butter, and when cheese is used fish has been given as an alternative to meat as an accompaniment.

One day I should like to be a first-class cook, and I've had daydreams about retiring to a restaurant or a monastery kitchen. But I haven't become one yet. In the religious life I have often had more help from second-class saints, mystics who never made it, and spiritual wobblers, than from the truly great, the first class and the perfect. The former were close enough to learn from – the latter seemed to inhabit a different reality. If this book helps you in the same way then I am content.

Conversion helps

oz/lb/grammes (approximate)

1oz   is 25g
4oz (¼lb)   is 100g

but as these are only approximate

8oz (½lb)   is 225g
16oz (1lb)   is 450g

1 kilo is about 2¼lb

Cups across the Atlantic

A British cup holds 10 fluid oz
  which is ½ an Imperial pint (20 fluid oz)

but

An American cup holds 8 fluid oz
  which is ½ an American pint (16 fluid oz)

An Imperial pint is about a ½ litre
  or 2½ American cups

An American cup holds just over a ¼lb of flour
  and just under ½lb of sugar

Spoons

A level Tablespoon holds
  about ½oz of flour or cocoa
  or about 1oz of sugar, butter or rice

American spoons are a little smaller than
  British ones

Ovens

	Fahrenheit	Gas	Centigrade (approximate)
	250	½	120
Cool	275	1	140
	300	2	150
Moderate	325	3	160
	350	4	180
Moderately hot	375	5	190
	400	6	200
Hot	425	7	220
	450	8	230
Very hot	475	9	240

Contents

17

APPETIZERS AND STARTERS

There are a lot of appetizers in this book because I was brought up on them. My mother spent a long time in hospital when I was a child and I was partly raised by my Russian and Polish grandparents. They had a great deal of love but no sense of time. In the kitchen there was a long buffet and a samovar which never went out, even on the Sabbath. Meals were leisurely, haphazard affairs, like an unending cocktail party. When we could afford it, which was not often, there were actually cocktails too – like vodka sucked through a lump of sugar – lemon tea with rum was served at a 'literarish glayzel tay'. Then the local intelligentsia used to gather together to discuss art and revolution (sex would have shocked the radicals as much as my grandmother). Tough criticism of rabbis was encouraged, flippancy about the Deity was not.

I had a shock when I was evacuated. I suddenly found out that you had to eat at certain times and go to sleep at certain times, and that children were seen but not heard – which outraged me as I was a garrulous infant and a snob. It was like living in corsets, and I never really adjusted to it.

A gentleman came to see me. He was prosperous and had obviously succeeded in life. His coat had that shiny, but not too shiny look of real camel hair, and his after-shave didn't come from the supermarket. His tie firmly pointed out (but discreetly of course) that it was conceived in Paris.

His surname was right too, and my only wonder was that it wasn't hyphenated, like up-market candidates in local elections. His Schaeffer pen waved over the form I had given him to fill out.

I looked over his shoulder to check up that all was well, and my eye glanced at the address he had given as his place of birth. Well, well – so he was born in Stepney!

I suddenly asked him where, because I was born there too. 'Oh, you wouldn't know the street,' he replied. 'It was not very significant.'

He named it, we looked at each other, and suddenly burst into laughter. We knew each other only too well.

Before we were separated by the evacuation we had tied street knockers together, and had climbed up gas lamp-posts to see if we could find out how to turn them on. (Thank God we never did.) We had hung around the crash doors of the local cinema, and thrown peanut shells at the enraged manager. We had sat on the kerb huddled together, eating one portion of chips between us, sodden with vinegar, and dotted with gobs of salt. We had tried to mingle our blood, pirate fashion, with a rusty kitchen knife.

'Fancy you becoming a Rabbi!' he said.

'And you becoming a tycoon,' I added.

I reminded him that in our childhood we had not been entirely irreligious. We had done the round of synagogues on Sabbath.

Most of them gave the good children a little taste of ritual wine, and if you hopped it smartly from one to the other, you could chalk up a glassful before their generosity dried up.

We had also slithered into Jewish weddings and confirmations, and been given a cream cake or a piece of herring before being thrown out.

We had finally been separated after catapulting a toffee into our teacher's throat as he was showing us how to chant scripture.

And in our conversation the companions of our childhood were resurrected in our memory, as surely as the prayers in the liturgy promise. There was the mad lady at the corner of the street, who threw buckets of water at the horses, because she saw her parents killed by Cossacks. There was the Jewish man who had converted, and walked the streets more lonely than anyone else I knew, preaching his newfound faith. (We were told to stop our ears lest we became converted too). There was the miracle Rabbi down the street who never left his house or room, and the Salvation Army ladies gently preaching their message of 'blood and fire' through the excited streets.

When we were good – which was not often despite our dissembling – we were given 'Chopped Liver Pâté' on thick slices of fresh white bread. It's very simple to make, and perfect for a summer lunch.

Jewish chopped liver pâté

Serves 4 as a generous starter;
8 as a party dish
1 large onion
¾–1lb chicken livers
5 eggs, hard-boiled
1 thick slice fresh white
bread
1oz chicken fat or margarine
pinch sugar
salt, pepper to taste

Chop onion and fry it in a generous amount of chicken fat or margarine (I add a pinch of sugar to help it brown).

Clean the chicken livers, removing any discoloured bits, and add to the pan and brown them.

Mince the contents including the fat with 4 hard-boiled eggs and one thick slice of fresh white bread (without crusts). Salt and pepper to taste, and chill. Chop the remaining hard-boiled egg and sprinkle over the top.

Fresh pepper does make a difference here. Turkey livers give a different flavour but are very nice too. It can be eaten straight away.

If you want to keep it, then seal it with a covering of melted chicken fat or margarine.

You can make a vegetarian version substituting frozen sliced green beans cooked *al dente* in place of the livers, fried in a highly flavoured and seasoned vegetarian fat.

Past glories (sort of)

When I was a bishop (sort of) of a bankrupt diocese, I was received in considerable state on arrival. Sometimes a car awaited me, and a chauffeur sat in it, and he took off his cap when he saw me. The Chairman, President or Bishop (not sort of but real) whom I met treated me with a respect utterly out of proportion to the tiny Jewish survivor communities I represented. They represented the powers that be, and I represented (sort of) the God of Israel.

It was very comfortable and luxurious. The only previous times I had sat in the back of chauffeur-driven cars were always in a hearse on my way to a funeral. There was the chauffeur, the coffin and me, but the conversation lacked sparkle.

But in between these high encounters life was a little different. I had a long title it was true, but not much money to back it up. So I took cheap trains around Europe, sometimes slept in railway waiting-rooms, even hitch-hiked here and there hiding my robes, and I thoroughly enjoyed myself.

The trains I travelled in broke down, which was only fair as you get what you pay for in this life as well as the next. When a train breaks down, two things can happen. If the Holy Ghost keeps away, the atmosphere turns nasty, and people shove, push and complain. If the Holy Ghost comes along for the ride, you can have the loveliest spontaneous parties in a railway siding somewhere in Central Europe.

An elderly lady once sang us a song when we got stuck in a snowdrift in Germany. She had been a singer at the time of the First World War, and the words she sang were all about regrets, and violets. She was shy but overcame it, and she inspired an Austrian to unlock his sausage-shaped case. It was the only time I have heard a trombone solo. In a confined railway carriage it makes a powerful noise, and I only recovered two towns later.

On the train we ate whatever we could find – chewing-gum, cheese, and bananas squashed against the sauerkraut. In society I ate smoked salmon and elegant appetizers, of which this was one. It is a dish fit for the eminent, and certainly more than fit for any roving clergyman you might encounter in a snowdrift in central Germany.

Snob salmon

Steam the fresh salmon. Remove any skin and bones, and flake it. Cut up the smoked salmon pieces into small bits, and mix both fresh and smoked salmon together with the soft melted butter, 1 Tablespoon of olive oil and a beaten egg yolk. Let it chill in the fridge overnight.

It is very rich, and you can drink iced vodka with it, as you reminisce about Tsarskoye-Selo and the glories of St Petersburg.

Serves 6
½lb salmon, fresh or frozen
¼lb smoked salmon
¼lb butter
1 Tablespoon olive oil
1 egg yolk

Playing safe!

I like cooking at the table, but I am wary of it. I feel happier if it is your table not mine, and then I can sit back and weep over the ruins like Jeremiah.

I shall never forget the time I tried to rescue a dull dinner party by flambéing bananas in brandy. The flames singed the eyelashes of a lady who wanted to see into the pan. She got an eyeful, for one of her eyelashes fell off and burnt merrily in the brandy.

The smell was dreadful, and if you decide to burn your vanities, do not do so at dinner. It is ascetic but unsocial. There is of course another lesson to be drawn from this episode – do not wear false eyelashes when you have not examined the menu.

At another party we were served *Fondue bourguignonne.* We were given long forks and a mound of little bits of steak, and there was a pan of hot oil in the middle of the table.

Led by our hostess we skewered the meat, dipped it into the oil, then into chutney and relish, and then into our mouths. One lady burnt her tongue and shrieked, '*C'est le goût de l'enfer, hein?*' This we agreed by little nods was hard on our hostess.

But as the train of disaster developed like a Greek tragedy, we pondered that little shriek. I dipped my bit of meat, but someone stabbed at it too, and while we smiled at each other politely, our forks fenced for possession.

The steak dropped off into the oil, and lay there cooking until its smell recalled the burnt offerings of my ancestors. When the oil went off the boil, the meat got sodden.

When the oil boiled over, it took the bloom off the French polish. Now some people do manage it beautifully, but if you are new to the game, practise on your family before you experiment on friends.

Here is something very safe, and like many good people not as dull as it or they may seem.

Eggs and spring onions

Boil the eggs for 9 minutes, shell them and while they are hot, chop them and mix them with the butter. Now with a pair of scissors chop the green parts of a whole bunch of spring onions. Stir them into the chopped eggs. Salt and pepper (freshly ground if possible) to taste. Don't under-season, and you have to chill the paste in a fridge overnight and serve with thin toast. If you want to make it more exotic, chop in some coriander leaves.

Serves 6
10 eggs
3oz butter
1 bunch spring onions
fresh coriander leaves (optional)
salt, pepper

Delights of store-gazing

I had come to the end of my holiday. My bags were packed, and I was ready to go, but the plane was delayed for eight or nine hours. I had an extra day to enjoy myself, but no money to enjoy it with, for I had spent the lot.

In many countries culture is quite costly, so museums were out. I sat down in a park and considered the matter. The best things in life are free – but what are they?

Instead of museums, I decided to go on a tour of supermarkets. I chose three and intended to spend just under an hour in each. I

24

discovered treasures I had never known before.

Do you know you can buy liquid smoke? It comes in tubes like toothpaste. You can also aerosol your frying-pan with cooking oil, to give it the thinnest of coatings.

One supermarket had a collection of soya sauces – more than 20 varieties – which held me spellbound.

When I walked along the streets, I looked in the shop windows with fresh eyes, because I didn't want to buy. I became fascinated with the dummies in the store windows – the ones which show off clothes. Have you ever inspected them, the hussies! Why do they look down at you? What are they sneering about, and why so superior? In one window, they looked so malevolent, I backed away.

If you don't believe me, inspect the shops in your high street.

My last port of call was the meditation and prayer room at the airport. It was between the diamond counter and the VIP lounge, so it was only for upmarket spirituality.

Had anyone but me ever been there? From the suspicious amazed look of the guards, apparently not. I tried to pray, but I kept thinking of things to eat, for I was now hungry.

Next time I shall be prepared with some oatmeal biscuits and this savoury onion pâté.

Onion and parsley pâté

Serves 6
10 eggs
4 Tablespoons chopped parsley
2 large onions, chopped
3oz margarine
4 Tablespoons oil
1 teaspoon sugar
salt, freshly ground pepper

Hardboil the eggs, shell them, and chop them. Fry one onion in the margarine and oil. Sprinkle the frying onions with the sugar so that they brown.

Chop the second, raw onion finely. Mix the eggs, both sorts of onions, the parsley and the fat in the pan all together. Season well with salt and freshly ground pepper. Leave it for several hours in the fridge to blend.

Don't worry about the smell of the onions. Places of worship are not museums, they are for life and its realities.

Likes and dislikes

A famous author once came clean and wrote two articles. The first was about the great books which never influenced him – this list was headed by Shakespeare – and the books which had influenced him. At the top of the second list was Rider Haggard, whom few of us have taken seriously since childhood.

This set me pondering about the things I ought to like and the things I actually like.

In an idle moment (yes, in the early hours of the morning) I started drawing up lists – and found out I wasn't at all the person I thought I was.

To my annoyance I was not so sophisticated as I thought. The things I do like are very simple.

Here are some of my likes: I like books with happy endings and I want to be sure the endings are happy before I begin. By 'happy' I don't mean anything exalted. I want the characters to end up married, well off, and preferably living on the Riviera. This of course rules out *Hamlet*, *Macbeth*, *King Lear* and most great literature. *Tant pis!*

I like riding the buses – especially routes I've never tried before. At the end of the line I find a café and chat to someone about life, secure in the knowledge that our intimacy will not last longer than two toasted tea-cakes and a Bakewell tart.

I like sitting in churches and synagogues which are empty. I like this especially on my way back from work. I don't mind being accosted by beggars, but I don't like being chatted-up by well-meaning clergy seeking souls.

I like bottled sauces and tinned pilchards (there go the shreds of my gastronomic reputation).

And now for some of the things I don't like. I don't like moody people at breakfast. That is not exactly true. I like them but they defeat me and I get dragged down too.

I don't like my second course being served at restaurants before I've finished the first.

I don't like the expression 'in this day and age'. One is quite enough.

I don't like it when people start off by saying 'Do you mind if I'm frank . . . ?' Yes, I do mind, because what comes after is usually malicious.

I don't like being manipulated.

But I had better end on a cheerful note – and with me that is usually food.

This is an appetizer which I didn't like at first, but I grew to like more and more as I got adjusted to it, and I adjusted it to my own taste. It is Hummus, the chick-pea paste which can be found in any café in the Eastern Mediterranean. It is, alas, one of the few things which unite such diverse countries as Greece, Turkey, Lebanon, Israel and Egypt. It contains a lot of protein, and is very little trouble to make if you have a processor.

I no longer bother to cook the chick-peas. Tins of them are readily available and not exorbitant. This is a recipe for a 1lb tin of chick-peas.

Hummus

Serves 4–6

Break up the bread and process this with the chick-peas, oil, lemon juice, Tahini, garlic, parsley, Garam Masala, sugar, chili pepper and half the coriander.

Adjust flavours, and spread out on a platter.

Decorate with the remaining coriander, black olives, and a little oil.

Serve with good fresh bread and hot pitta.

If the paste is too wet then process in some more wholemeal bread. This firms it up, and gives it a nutty flavour.

1lb tin chick-peas (including liquid)
2 slices wholemeal bread with crusts
1 Tablespoon oil (olive, if you can afford it)
1 Tablespoon lemon juice
1 Tablespoon Tahini (sesame paste)
1 clove garlic
1 Tablespoon chopped parsley
1 teaspoon Garam Masala
½ teaspoon sugar
pinch chili pepper
2 Tablespoons freshly chopped coriander leaves
6 black olives
salt to taste

Just after the war ended I used to take a rucksack to school on the last day of term. The moment school ended, I started out on a journey to the continent. Quite often I walked, but quite often people gave me lifts. I think I learnt more about human beings in those holidays than I acquired in all the years since.

People are really very kind. The unlikeliest vehicles used to stop for me on French country roads and take me a few more kilometres. I travelled in peasant donkey-carts, on a fire-engine and on a moving haystack. One honeymoon couple stopped for me and, after a half day's journey, invited me to join them for a week on their honeymoon – why I never knew. They were very sweet and called me formally 'Monsieur' for the whole time. The young bride gave me my first lessons in French cooking.

I learned a lot of theology from a jovial priest in a dusty cassock, who stopped on his little motor-bike while I was peering out of a hedge. How the two of us ever got moving on that little machine with my enormous rucksack I still don't understand. Faith must have had a lot to do with it, for he kept on taking his hand off the bars while he gave me an impassioned account of worker priests and sacramental theology. Even now as I try to think of those subjects in French, they are accompanied by the 'bang bang' of Thérèse – his little machine.

I had just seen my first French films, and when a young lady agreed to dance a twirling French waltz with me to a little three-piece band I gave a sigh of contentment. As the saxophone, piano and drums jerked away I knew this was romance. How gentle was the music compared to today's heavy metal, how innocent our feelings!

My first contact with the Catholic church came at this time. In some provincial town I developed an abscess on my tooth. I had no money and was exhausted by pain. Some Capuchins took me in. They wanted to learn English, but all I had with me was a copy of *Ulysses* by James Joyce, and a dictionary. We translated the missal into English, and James Joyce into French and Italian. What they learned from it, I wonder. But I learned from them the beautiful flavour of the religious life with its great pools of quiet and its dignified poverty.

Since I always associate foods with periods in my life, I associate poverty, chastity and obedience with tomatoes. We ate them every day with rough baked bread, onions and oil.

Here is a much fancier tomato dish which a friend of mine, the yacht designer Kim Holman, invented. When tomatoes are cheap it is worth serving at a dinner party because it is refreshing and delicate.

Cold tomato soufflé

Serves 8
4 eggs
1lb tomatoes
2 teaspoons castor sugar
approx. ½oz gelatine
salt, pepper, lemon juice to taste
basil (optional)

Separate the eggs. Now skin the tomatoes. (The best way I know is to nick the skins, plunge them in boiling water, and then slip the skins off.) Put them in a blender, pips and all. Gently heat the tomato mush with the castor sugar, add salt, pepper and lemon juice to taste. Remove from heat and stir in the gelatine. When the gelatine has dissolved add the mush to the egg yolks and beat. Then fold in gently the beaten egg whites. Spoon the soufflé into ramekins and chill.

This is the original version. I add some basil to the tomatoes to remind me of the dusty roads of Southern France and wayside picnics in Italy.

An eye for trouble

In my work I have to speak to a lot of people with problems. I am not a marriage guidance counsellor, and the only therapy I know comes from being the receiver of it – not the giver. So I have no special skills or powers of discernment, and I am not the person to fly to in such situations.

In other words, if I had that sort of problem I wouldn't go to me to get myself out of it. But over the years I can at least spot the sort of situation or remark which leads nowhere.

There is the 'Do you love me as much as I love you?' tangle. If you answer yes or no to that one, you're wrong. The only possibility is to lob it back. As there is no accurate barometer of love, both parties come away feeling cheated and aggrieved.

The next trap concerns the interpretation of words unsaid. I was once walking down Whitechapel High Street. A large Jewish lady marched ahead followed by the forlorn remains of her husband.

'Don't speak to me,' she said.

The dejected husband said nothing.

'I'm not listening,' she added.

Again a dejected silence.

'Quiet!' she said.

Again nothing.

It was a very instructive conversation or monologue.

Another potential source of disaster comes from seeing too many films or soap operas. Even as a child, I noticed that the emotional temperature of my family shot up after they had all gone to see a Bette Davis weepie.

Instead of having a normal row, they registered agony, and smiling-through-tears and all that sort of stuff. They were also inclined to

little scenarios of rejection. 'If you don't make me Horlicks, I shall walk out and never come back. You treat me like dirt.'

The trouble with that routine was that if the person did walk out, somebody had to swallow their words very quickly. It is dangerous mixing a sense of theatre with real life.

Another ploy which could easily backfire was the emotional blackmail drama. For this you had to start with 'How could you?' But then it had to be accompanied by effects. You had to wring your hands convincingly, which is actually rather difficult to do if you are not Bette Davis, and some tears (quality rather than quantity) were essential. Being caught with half an onion was shaming.

I think it is essential to have some favourite foods to put things to rights in any marriage. Few wives can resist an éclair, but do make sure it is real cream. And few husbands aren't softened by hot salt beef on rye-bread with mustard.

Now this pâté is tasty enough to satisfy him, and delicate enough to satisfy her, (or the other way round if they are not into role playing).

Reconciliation fish pâté

Mince into a soufflé dish the cod and haddock fillets, mixed with the bread. Mix into it the carrot, leek, parsnip, and celeriac, all grated finely. Separate the eggs. Add the beaten yolks into the fish and vegetable mixture. Beat the whites till stiff. Fold into the mixture with the sour cream, salt and pepper.

Put the soufflé dish in a pan of hot water and bake in a preheated oven for 1¼ hrs (300°F Gas 2 150°C). Serve warm.

Serves 6 as a main course, 8 for generous starters

1lb (cod and haddock) fillets, skinned
1 thick slice of white bread, without crusts
1 carrot
1 leek
½ parsnip
½ celeriac root
4 eggs
½ pint sour cream
2 teaspoons salt
½ teaspoon pepper

Festive fare on your own

A priest recently told me that more people came to him depressed at Christmas than at any other time, and they weren't just people spending it on their own, but married couples with or without children, and young people too.

I think it's because everybody is telling us what we ought to feel, and we may not feel that way at all. Radio, TV, the newspapers, and the cards are screaming at us: Enjoy, enjoy! Be merrier and merrier! Lose yourselves in a cloud cuckooland of plastic reindeer, White Christmas and indigestion.

If you *are* spending Christmas on your own, my first advice is, don't get bullied by the media. An awful lot of the merriment covers a lot of awful depression. Everyone has problems – that's life – including 'happy families'. The cheer covers people's problems, it doesn't solve them.

So if you feel reflective or nostalgic, then accept your feelings. I know for myself, a few tears are often necessary and they give me an appetite.

If I'm being honest, I want food which doesn't take much trouble to prepare, which I can eat in an armchair, and which doesn't involve much washing-up. I don't like being imprisoned in my own room. People want to be able to get out, and look at the Christmas crowds.

Celeriac and mustard dressing

Celeriac grated and marinated in a sweet mustardy French dressing overnight. You don't have to cook the celeriac.

1 large root celeriac
dressing:
1 cup oil (olive and corn oil mixed)
½ cup lemon juice
2 teaspoons English mustard
3 teaspoons sugar
¾ teaspoon salt
¼ teaspoon pepper

Scrambled eggs with smoked salmon

Eggs scrambled with cream, with smoked salmon cut up and stirred in just as they are setting.

In food as in prayer you have to come clean. If you try to be somebody you're not, then you'll end up as artificial as the canned kindness of the commercials, and as forlorn as the merry smiles glued on sad people. Be yourself! That's how God created you!

Packaged for travel

A lot of my friends make it very clear to me that their holidays, unlike mine, are free range. They go off to obscure places on the edge of the Sahara to get away from it all, and then return with obscure stomach illnesses better left unnamed. They take boats without stabilizers to islands (well, rocks really) on which they perch eating oatmeal, until the next boat limps its way through the tidal bore. Some cheat by basking on a beach in Bulgaria (all incl.) and making it sound like *The Scarlet Pimpernel.*

Another lot are free spirits who despise any hotel – even ones rejected by all the package tours. They sigh and save for a second home which must be away from it all. It is so far that it takes two weeks to get to it, and two weeks to get away from it. So they can never get to it, until they are retired and too tired and decrepit to make it.

Their Shangri-las have superb views as they are situated on top of vertical mountains, or clinging to a cliff face. No buses go there, and you have to pay a native driver danger money to deliver you at the front door. The sunsets are magnificent, but you can't eat them, and what happens if you can't find a tin-opener or have just run out of baked beans? You aren't a Sherpa!

I myself endure the insults, and go packaged like everyone else.

I am writing this sitting by the side of a pool. At my side there is lemon juice laced with gin, and a Bible in Spanish. (The best way to learn a language is to read the Psalms in it.) 'O taste and see that the Lord is good,' it says (Psalm 34) and tonight I eat fish and veg. Spanish style. But my fish is not embalmed in batter, which is a pity as I enjoy it with lots of vinegar and salt. It is tasty though and Costa-ish, and this is the recipe for the veg. which goes with it.

Ratatouille

In a large casserole heat the oil. Put the ingredients in, in the following order, leaving a few minutes between the stages.

1. chopped onion and garlic
2. aubergines and courgettes and peppers (all sliced with skin)
3. chopped tomatoes and sugar
4. vinegar, salt, pepper (freshly ground) and herbs
5. cook for a further 20 minutes

If you eat it cold, serve it with lemon portions for the diners to squeeze.

Serves 4

½lb onions
1lb tomatoes
2 medium aubergines
3 cloves garlic
2 sweet peppers (green)
6 courgettes
1 cup olive oil
4 Tablespoons white wine vinegar
1 teaspoon sugar
Mixed herbs (fresh if possible, dried if not): parsley, thyme, oregano, basil, bay leaf
2 lemons
salt and pepper, freshly ground

Northern lights

Rain is depressing but snow is not, provided you are not too old, too poor or too isolated. The day begins with magic. There is the white gleaming light reflected from the snow, the hoar frost on the window, and the dogs race through the drifts, intoxicated with snow madness.

I was intoxicated with snow madness too, and I went skiing in northern latitudes at night. They strapped a lamp on my head, and we all pushed off. Ahead of us was a clear sheet of snow, and beyond that a sparkling forest. I glided triumphant to the horizon. I missed the first tree, and I missed the second.

When I woke up 30 hours later they gave me soup to rebuild my strength and a small but vital bone. They don't talk much in Scandinavia and during my convalescence they said it with herrings.

I ate them salted, pickled and raw, in mustard sauce, wine sauce and tomato sauce. Sometimes the herrings wore their heads and sometimes they took them off for the decapitated look.

There is an awful lot of nature over there but not much small talk.

The only animated subject of conversation I remember was land-slides or rather snowslides (with boulders). It seemed that one's nearest and dearest were prone to them.

Piles of boulders were pointed out to me on occasion, with a sad but factual comment that Auntie lived there. All I could say was 'sorry' which seemed inadequate, but then I did not know Auntie before the snowslide.

Let us turn to the herring instead. It is a cheerier subject.

Scandinavian hors-d'oeuvre

For each person, put a raw egg yolk in the centre of a saucer. Around it in separate concentric circles arrange the chopped raw onion, chopped anchovy fillets, potatoes, cut up little titbits of Gafelbitter herring and chopped dill cucumbers. Sprinkle a little cayenne pepper over the egg yolk, and a little paprika over the potatoes. Eat with toast or hot bread, mixing in the chopped bits with the yolk.

Serves 4
4 yolks of egg, raw
1 large Spanish onion, chopped
2oz tin anchovy fillets
2 large waxy potatoes, boiled
4oz tin of Gafelbitter herring*
4 medium dill cucumbers, chopped
cayenne, paprika to taste

* You can buy it in tins from Scandinavia.

Thoughts sacred and profane

I live in a Greek area of London. Plucking up my courage, I went into the Greek church which is not far from the bottom of my road. I was overwhelmed.

A great mosaic of Christ glowed from the roof, and around me was the company of heaven, a glorious throng of apostles, saints and martyrs in glowing red and blue tunics, dazzling in their gold cloaks. Candles glinted in the darkness, the priest chanted quietly and some devout ladies concentrated on their prayers.

I began to understand how the Russian envoys who were searching for a religion felt when they came into Santa Sophia at Constantino-ple – it seemed to them they were in heaven itself.

It's a different feeling in a synagogue. There are no images, and you look towards the symbols and teachings of heaven – the ark and the eternal light. You look towards it, you are not surrounded by it.

It was a moving sensation in the church and since I felt it I can begin to understand something of Orthodox spirituality.

Around the church there is an enchanting Greek and Cypriot life. The grocery shops are cosy places, family-run, with a lot of chit-chat. You can buy about 20 types of olive, and delicious sheets of the finest pastry, which you bake with almonds and syrup.

The little cafés are intensely alive and human. Greek food is tasty and often classically simple. It is always served with the exhilaration of a party, and such a sauce cannot be imitated.

Aubergine pâté

Serves 4 as a generous starter;
8 as a party dish

1 medium aubergine
1 Tablespoon mayonnaise
1 Tablespoon lemon juice
3 cloves garlic, crushed
½ teaspoon salt
½ teaspoon sugar
¼ teaspoon pepper
2 eggs, hard-boiled and chopped
tomatoes and olives to garnish

Prick the aubergine with a sharp knife (to avoid an aubergine explosion from the heat). Then put it under a hot grill for 15–20 mins or bake in a hot oven for double the time. (I prefer baking as it is easier, but the grilling gives a smokier taste.) You'll know the aubergine is baked when it is soft all over, as you prick it with a fork. Cool. Cut in half and scoop out the inside. Mash the aubergine with a fork (if you haven't got a food processor or blender). Add the remaining ingredients. Garnish with sliced tomatoes and/or olives.

You can vary this by omitting the mayonnaise and egg, and adding 1 Tablespoon of Tahini (crushed sesame-seed paste) and more lemon juice to taste.

Serve this aubergine pâté with Greek bread – either pitta, or the sesame-seed loaves. It will delight all the lovers of Greek islands, dark little cafés, and the eastern Med.

Safe but sure

In my childhood going to a hotel or a boarding-house was an adventure. Neither the comfort nor the discomfort was standard. On the one hand you had your shoes cleaned, even in boarding-houses. On the other you were a hero if you made it to the bathroom, even in hotels (people ponged more then!).

Strange gales blew round corners, lights were dim and corridors vast. The carpet was definitely not all-in, only a thin strip to indicate your path – like a clue in a treasure hunt, or like the children of Israel crossing the Red Sea.

When and if you made it, the bathroom was occupied and you queued. You stood behind haughty ladies who wore great paper-clips in their hair, with smears of cold cream on their faces.

The men in the queue were shaggy in hairy flannel pyjamas. You were all frozen with embarrassment or cold.

Modern hotels are, of course, much more comfortable physically. But spiritually they are often barren beyond belief. Despite the TV and the air-conditioning, it is like living in an airport. There is the same sense of being nowhere.

Many people today solve their holiday problem by exchanging homes. There is an excitement about stepping into other people's homes and other people's lives, and poking into their kitchen drawers (it's quite fair, because they're doing the same to you).

In somebody else's kitchen though, it is best to keep to dishes which don't require advanced technology. I steer clear of foreign pressure-cookers and strange microwave ovens.

I did spend a happy weekend with the machine which trimmed radishes into roses or did so for everyone else except me.

The following recipe is versatile, because it can be made with an axe (my grandmother) or a mincer (my mother) or a food processor (me). My grandmother used to mumble in Yiddish as she wielded her great chopper. As you won't know her incantations nor are you wearing her safety amulets, I suggest you avoid the axe, for the sake of your fingers.

Chop and mix together all the ingredients, reserving some egg for garnish. Do not use any of the pickling liquid from the herrings, for it will be too sharp.

Fork the chopped herring in a thin layer on to a platter. Scatter with more chopped hard-boiled egg – it takes away the sad grey look, which should not put you off, as it is delicious.

Eat with good-quality white bread or Jewish Cholla bread.

Serves 4 as a generous starter;
8 as a party dish

3 pickled herrings (the rollmop type), without their tails, but don't worry about their skins

3 slices brown bread, decrusted, soaked in water and squeezed very dry

3 eggs, hard-boiled

3 slices pickled onion from the herring jar, or raw onion

1 large dessert apple, peeled and cored

1 Tablespoon salad oil

1 teaspoon sugar
1 teaspoon salt } **or to taste**
½ teaspoon pepper

I am sure it would look very nice with radish roses too but my holiday ended before I mastered the art.

BEAUTIFUL SOUP

I have a friend who makes Garbage Soup. Each week she clears out the vegetable rack and the fridge and (with discretion) boils and purées the lot with judicious additions. The result is delicious 'Garbage'. It is never the same twice, it provides a good conversation piece as family and guests try to guess the contents, but even if you are more orthodox, liquidized soups have solid advantages. You can prepare them well in advance, they are cheap, and extendable so that you don't have to worry about portions, and as you only need one pot and a spoon there isn't much washing up. In my childhood thick soups like a meal went out of favour, but the new generation is compost-conscious and likes lumps floating in earthy colours. The ideal has changed from tasteful chintz at a 'Troc' tea dance to oatmeal-coloured gruel bowls at teach-ins.

I also like iced soups, but not fruit soups which disconcert me. The only soup I do not like is cold beer soup. I enjoy stews with boiling beer, but I cannot stomach it flat and tepid from a soup plate. Iced soups are simple. Cooked frozen peas or broccoli or cauliflower whizzed in a blender are tasty and easy, and more than that if you improve them with fresh mint, or garden herbs, with chopped raw onion or garlic, and cream.

Mm – smells of GARBAGE...

So this is a compliment?

'Szcz' not in front of children

My grandparents spoke only Polish when they didn't want me to listen in. So though I picked up a wide vocabulary as a child most of it is unsuitable for polite conversation, and of no use to me at all, if I should ever meet the Pope, which I admit is unlikely. He is not going to say, 'Rabbi, what striking words you know!' and egg me on. On the other hand in the pictures I've seen of him, there is a smile lurking at the corner of his lips, so I wonder.

I might be able to muster up some kitchen Polish, and with a bit of pointing, and a lot of tasting, there might be some 'relevant process of meaningful communication between us' as the highstepping media diplomats have it. I would smile in welcome and say 'Barszcz', and he would know that this was a soup, not a warning.

At least he would know it, if I pronounced my *szcz* correctly. I am out of practice now, so why don't you try it instead. Go Polish – stand in front of the mirror, and say 'szcz' clearly and distinctly, while watching your mouth movements carefully.

Yes, it is a little difficult I know, but do it again and again. Practice makes perfect, and you never know when you are going to need a talent like that. There you go. Szcz – SZCZ – szcz – SZcz – szCZ. When you are better at it, you can emphasize the first 'Z'. Later on, I might teach you some words. There's temptation for you! But if you are just no good at languages, and can't pronounce it, then you can drink some Barszcz instead and eat your words – which may be easier, and if they are my grandparents' words, much safer.

My grandmother made Cabbage Barszcz and Beetroot Barszcz. She had an iron cauldron, and used so many cracked bones that her kitchen looked like an ancient battlefield or a rich archaeological dig. She died many years ago and so did her cauldron. It was blown up in the blitz which was typical, there was always something grisly about it.

Since I do not intend to watch over a cauldron of seething bones for hour after hour, while keening away in medieval Polish, I have a more up-to-date version, and I no longer have to look like an extra for the witches' scene in *Macbeth*.

This recipe goes very well served as an accompaniment to Polish cauliflower (see p. 92) and Polish herring salad (p. 108).

Beetroot borsht or barszcz

In a blender or food processor blend 4 beetroots (chopped), the garlic, bouillon, single cream, and yoghourt. If you blend the beetroot at first with only a little stock and add more liquid through the funnel, you get a smoother mixture. Blend in the juice of half a lemon, castor sugar, and salt to taste. Adjust lemon juice and sugar to taste.

Serve it cold in bowls, with side-dishes of cooked beetroot, hard-boiled eggs, cold boiled potatoes, green of spring onions (all chopped) and sour cream dusted with paprika. People mix their helpings from the side-dishes into their Barszcz or Borsht.

Anyway, however you pronounce it, it makes a lovely summer lunch.

As you stir the red mixture, don't forget to repeat 'szcz' in time. Put a mirror over your kitchen table and you can watch your mouth.

Serves 4–6
5 medium beetroots, cooked
1 clove garlic
½ pint bouillon or light stock
¼ pint single cream
¼ pint yoghourt
½ lemon
1 dessertspoon castor sugar
salt
4 large potatoes
1 bunch spring onions
½ pint sour cream
4 eggs, hard-boiled
paprika

There are many other delights in a Polish kitchen. You can make pâté out of mushrooms. You can stuff little dumplings with meat and watch them bob up temptingly in your soup. You can make your strudel with poppy seeds, and you can cook goose and duck in more ways than you will ever remember.

You can start on all this after you have done your homework. So get on with it. Pronounce after me 'szcz, SZCZ, SZcz, szCZ' just as they do in old 'Szczezin'.

Nil desperandum!

There are certain situations which are beyond redemption, where all who enter abandon hope because there is nothing else they can do.

Sailing is rich in such situations. At one time I and my friends were heavy smokers. We were good companions who made our way across the North Sea without temper or cross words, despite the fog, drizzle and bloody-mindedness of that uncomfortable stretch of water. We gazed at each other kindly, sucking away at our pipes and cigarettes and huddling into our waterproof coats.

Then, on one voyage we were five nautical miles out and found we had left the tobacco behind. It is difficult to describe the strain of that journey. We searched out old ash-trays and went through garbage bins for a stub abandoned in happier days. When this proved fruitless we tried to think of substitutes. We experimented with mixed herbs, cotton-wool, and Shredded Wheat. My advice is to eat your breakfast cereal, not smoke it.

I suppose it would have been worse if we had remembered the tobacco and forgotten the matches! Where can you find two flints to rub together near the Goodwin Sands?

Other tragedies are forgetting the tin-opener or losing the cork-screw. It's surprising what you can do to a tin without piercing it. You can jump on it, hammer it, thump it and saw it with the breadknife. Its shape alters, its resistance doesn't and there is blood everywhere.

The loss of a corkscrew is less urgent, but trying to excavate a cork with a table-fork is maddening when you are thirsty. One toughie I knew once told me to break the neck of the bottle and strain the glass through my teeth. But that must be a joke, and in any case I have gaps, so how would that help me?

The following simple, soothing and undramatic dish is just right for a boat or a caravan. Everything is cooked in one pot and there is no frying. As there is no grease and no strong seasoning, it will not make you queasy.

Undramatic fish chowder

Dice the onions and potatoes. Bring milk to simmer in a big pot. Add the onions. After a few minutes add the potatoes. When both are just soft, add fish fingers, cod or haddock (skinned and boned), cut into chunks. They will cook very quickly. Add salt and pepper to taste. When the fish is just cooked add a small tin of sweetcorn or Mexicorn (drained) and a small tin of peas (drained). Do not use the liquid from either – it will be too strong. Simmer so that every ingredient is heated through, and serve in bowls. Sometimes I add dried sweet peppers to the potatoes. They have a strong flavour, and make the chowder more colourful, though it looks quite nice already.

Serves 4 with repeats, 6 without
3 medium onions
3 large potatoes
2 pints milk
½–1lb cod, haddock, or fish
   fingers
1 tin sweetcorn or Mexicorn
   (sweetcorn with peppers)
1 small tin peas
2 Tablespoons dried sweet
   peppers (optional)
salt, pepper to taste

I never did like tragedies very much and have a sneaking sympathy with the Philistines of the eighteenth century who gave *King Lear* a happy ending.

Dark Spanish nights

I have just returned from Spain, and want to take the first flight back. I want to live in Malaga, and shop in the alleyways near the port, and drop into bars and churches, and drink sweet Spanish wine, and meditate a little. It's easier to get hold of sweet Spanish wine and a plate of anchovies than to meditate.

It is extraordinary, but all the places of worship seem to be shut. Do they wait till a lookout sees me, and then bolt the doors? Or are they always locked? Or perhaps they only cater for an élite spiritual clientèle who have a special devotion to the midnight office and none other will do.

Anyway, if I lived there long enough, and learnt more Spanish I could find out. I know the first few verses of the Spiritual Canticle of St John of the Cross by heart. It is powerful stuff, but it doesn't help me much in finding a chemist or avoiding a bullfight.

I tried to explain to the chemist that I had a hangover, but the only words at hand were about dark nights and desolation. These were accurate enough as far as I was concerned, but they puzzled him. Anyway he presented me with something for 'mystical migraine', and it was sticky, sweet and delicious like most Spanish medicines (so unlike our NHS) and I decided to live, and offer a prayer of thanksgiving – if anyone would ever let me in to say it, that is.

What I remember now from that dark night are some English mates, bowls of garlic soup, and English rugger songs which sounded quite Andalusian, and were applauded by the people in the bar. 'Was that a love song, *Señor*?' someone enquired, in Spanish. 'Er, *si, si*,' I replied.

Now here is the recipe for garlic soup. Don't weaken and cut down on the garlic, or you will only have insipid gravy. Just make sure that everyone has some, and you will be safe together.

Garlic soup (Anglo-Welsh-Spanish version)

Using a saucepan, fry 4 sliced cloves of garlic in the olive oil till brown. Cut up the potatoes and onion, and add, together with the remaining garlic (crushed), the stock, mixed herbs, and salt and pepper to taste.

Boil, and when all the vegetables are soft, mash with a potato masher. The mixture will be rough, like the rugger players I ate it with. They came from Wales and we sang rugger songs together.

Serves 8
8 cloves garlic
4 medium potatoes
1 large onion
2 pints light stock
2 Tablespoons olive oil
1 teaspoon mixed herbs
salt, freshly ground pepper

The soup we agreed goes very well with Welsh Rarebit, which I prefer to grated cheese scattered on top. Anyway this is an Anglo-Welsh-Spanish version and it is quite breathtaking.

If you munch a bunch of raw parsley it should get rid of the smell —
or so I was told. On the other hand I was also told

> That stinking goat on yonder hill
> Feeds all day long on Chlorophyll.

I never discovered who wrote these fascinating and informative
lines, but I take this chance to thank him or her.

Letting go

The most difficult thing in life is to let go. Tentacles of pride and
possession attach us to houses, people, pots and pans, and pen-
wipers.

All the débris of our life becomes precious and poignant in our
memory, whether or not it has any intrinsic merit. People get
sentimental over their fridges and freezers and toasters.

As we get older our minds become like our houses, so cluttered it is
difficult to move without smashing a memory.

But it is easier to let go of our objects than our feelings whether or
not the feelings have the slightest value. Pleasant memories recede
quickly to the horizon of our mind and cease to lure us from the
present. Painful memories clutch at us, so that we can scarcely let
them go. We are secretly in love with our own grief.

A Carmelite friar once told me to let my mind be like a sieve under
running water. Allow the bitterness and the pain to wash out of you,
he said, and drain away (that is what prayer is about). But the
strange thing is we even clutch at our bitterness. Perhaps we think
we wouldn't exist without it.

And the most difficult thing for me is to let go my sins and failures.
I go through a penitential period. I fast, and I pray like everyone else,
but often it doesn't work. My teacher at the seminary told me that
God forgives me. The Rabbis said forgiving is His profession, His
trade so to speak. My problem is that I find it hard to forgive myself.

Here is a recipe for Chilled cucumber soup which is fairly low on
calories, so I never have any regrets about it.

Chilled cucumber soup

Sauté the cucumbers and onion in the butter. Stir gently for about 10 minutes. Add the stock and continue cooking until the cucumber is soft, adding the tarragon, sugar, salt and pepper.

Blend the contents of the pan in a blender or processor and press through a sieve. Chill and serve sprinkled with chopped chives. Cream is optional. Cucumber is a delicate flavour and I prefer it concentrated.

Serves 4

2 cucumbers, washed and cut into chunks
1 onion, chopped
1oz butter
1 cup light stock
¼ teaspoon tarragon
½ teaspoon sugar
chopped chives
½ pint cream (optional)
salt, pepper

A shroud stain

I have a pretty shroud made for me by a fond aunt many years ago, when I first took the services for the Jewish Day of Atonement. It is made of fine white muslin, is trimmed with lace and has flounces on the cuffs and at the neck.

Pious Jews wear this garment at the important moments of their lives. Some wear it when they get married, some at the Passover meal. Most wear it on the Day of Atonement, when you pass a whole day (25 hours) 'out of this world', and all wear it when they die. It is white for purity, and because you are returning to God.

The Day of Atonement is rather like Lent, though it comes around September. It is a complete fast, and you shouldn't even brush your teeth. You can't handle money, do business, or write a letter. So people sit the whole day in the synagogue for non-stop prayers, and sermons.

People in the congregation sometimes say to me, 'How do you manage so much talk without food?' I, in turn, wonder at them. It seems to me easier to give sermons than to sit through them.

People have a substantial meal before the fast begins, and another when it ends. Some eat too much, and the result of their 'other worldliness' is indigestion. What I long for is a cup of strong and sweet tea. When you end a fast, you don't want anything too heavy, and I suggest this Gazpacho. You can make it in a liquidizer or blender, and it is very refreshing.

I learnt this recipe from Mrs Chani Smith, the wife of a fellow rabbi. She is a vegetarian, and a flautist. I did make Gazpacho before I met her, but her recipe is better than mine.

Mrs Smith's gazpacho

Blend together in a food processor or liquidizer, until smooth, the skinned tomatoes, cucumber, pepper, onion, garlic, eggs, tomato juice, vinegar, sugar, oil, salt and pepper. Chill. Pour into eight bowls, and garnish with chives and croutons.

Serves 8 penitents
5 tomatoes
1 cucumber, peeled, seeded and chopped
1 seeded green pepper, chopped
1 medium onion, chopped
2 cloves of garlic
4 raw eggs (size 3)
1 teacup tomato juice
¼ teacup vinegar (cider or wine vinegar)
¼ teacup olive oil
salt to taste
½ teaspoon sugar
pinch cayenne pepper

It is a colourful dish, as I know to my cost. I ate it after atoning and forgot to take off my shroud. My hand was unsteady, so there is a pinkish stain just below the lace, which never comes out with any washing. I hope my sins are less indelible.

An ascetic takes a greedy look

When I was a kid, I used to love reading success stories about young men (I identified like mad) who fought their way from rags to riches with a repulsive combination of virtue, luck and divine approval. Much later on in life, I am especially attracted to spiritual success stories about saints who fight their way to holiness through jungles, leprosy and prison camps. Both sorts of stories have many features in common though, as religious riches are material mud, I get a bit confused.

One's own character is such a puzzle. Here am I, a comfortable middle-aged rabbi, blessed with central heating, and a food processor, and aspiring to a microwave, devouring books on suffering, affliction and asceticism as I go to work in the morning.

I suck a bar of fruit-and-nut chocolate and read another chapter of that anorexic mystic Simone Weil. Everything she says seems so right.

I see, I feel the awful abyss that stretches between me and eternity, I suddenly begin to perceive my smallness, my nothingness (not even with a capital 'N'). I get upset, and I tuck into another bar of chocolate.

Then I think – yes all this is true, but there is something else in life as well. The same God who teaches me sacrifice and holiness also created chocolate bars and food processors and grace before meals and jokes that even make the downtrodden laugh.

So I offer you a taste of the good life.

If you are stepping out into this class of cooking, don't waver or lose your nerve. Yes, you will need butter. No, margarine will not do! What! You haven't got a bottle of Pernod handy? How remiss of you! Well the Lord created credit cards didn't He? So what are you waiting for? Yes, a whole pint of double cream. No, not evaporated milk!

You think you are too poor to be worldly with a recession on and all that. But even asceticism can be expensive, though it need not be. A holy nun I knew used to sleep on a peculiarly hard bed rather like a coffin. She had to give it up she told me when it wore out. Such beds cost too much. She got an ordinary cheap camp-bed instead. The simple life was just too expensive.

So without apologies here is a recipe I got from Super Chef Keith Simpson when he was at the Café St Pierre.

Cream of fennel soup, with Pernod and dill

Slice the onions and sauté in butter. Slice the fennel into four and add to the onions. Add the chicken stock, and a glass of Pernod or Ricard. Bring it all to the boil and simmer for an hour.

Now liquidize it and strain it and add the cream and, if you wish (I do wish), a further 2 glasses of Pernod. Correct seasoning and serve with a sprig of fresh dill on top. Never allow it to simmer after adding the cream.

Serves 8
1 head fennel
2 medium onions
4 pints chicken stock
1–3 schooners Pernod or Ricard
1 pint double cream
1oz butter
1 sprig fresh dill
salt, pepper

HEARTY EATING AND MAIN COURSES

I have not indulged in roasts in this section, because they do not fit my experience or my pocket. Meat for Jewish people is both complicated and expensive. After a steak, for example, has been soaked in salt water three times to remove the blood, all you can do with it is casserole it or braise it. Also cooking things in individual portions was never part of my early education, because there was too much poverty and charity around. (You never knew when another wave of refugees would come surging through your door.) My grandmother would have shaken with laughter at the sight of the pretty petite saucepans advertised in colour supplements. She went to work with a cauldron and an axe, which was her effective but simple processor. I have omitted or toned down many of the traditional delights of my childhood, as some of them were pretty grisly. My grandfather liked sucking the brains out of cooked carps' heads, while granny beamed at him, and the only roast I remember from childhood days was roast lung. It was like blotting paper or meaty foam. But it was not only cheap, it was giveaway. She also used to stuff chicken necks with savoury padding. The entire skin of the chicken was used to 'extend' the neck and I wondered as a child why chickens were constructed like giraffes.

But there were a lot of good things bubbling away in granny's cauldron too and I have tried to be faithful to her good taste if not to her exact ingredients.

I think my grandmother would have given a sigh of relief if she had been offered modern improvements. The affluent are sentimentalists not the poor. The lighter foods, and salads and clothes would have lightened her body and her spirits. She would also have traded her axe for a blender. I doubt though if she would have given up amulets. Life had taught her to be cautious, and she would have used them in conjunction with the NHS.

'Tis a bloody business

Watch yourself in men's kitchens for the knives are sharp and lethal. If you have to cook in one, locate sticking-plasters, blood staunchers, tourniquets, cottonwool buds, and iodine, before you begin. You will find them behind a plate with two bleeding steaks, and the Gentleman's Relish.

In men's kitchens, everything is hotter, saltier and unlabelled. That red powder is not paprika, it is chili. If by mistake you use it in a goulash, you will explode inside and feel like the Roman Empire ravaged by Attila.

Remember men use hot sauces, not the feeble fruity stuff you buy in brown bottles.

Be careful! Men use curry paste, not curry powder, and never curry-flavoured white sauce. They will have three types: Bangalore, Vindaloo, and Madras, i.e., fiery, burning, and very hot. Put lots of lager and a little water on the table. Make sure both are iced.

Men do not slap cold cream on their faces out of little pots. Their faces are too stubbly. Therefore they do not have lots of little pots you can put things in when empty.

What things? Well, a flake or two of tuna for example, 2 green olives and a black one, a tablespoon of yoghourt, 2 mint chocolates, or a dab of the original cold cream.

In men's kitchens there will be a large gin bottle on display, with some tonic in the fridge. You will not find a quarter bottle of crème-de-menthe hiding guiltily behind breakfast oats.

Men are partial to meat and mustard. Here is a 'macho' dish for hungry carnivorous males. They will be very happy with it because they can bang about, and tie knots, and hit things.

Ask your butcher to cut you four slices of meat for beef olives. He will probably cut them near the rump. With a meat tenderizer such as a mallet or rolling pin beat the slices until they are very thin (this will be good for your aggression). Cut each of them across into two.

Spread each slice with French mustard. At the thin end put a ½ tablespoon of raw Easy Cook Rice, ¼ of a hard-boiled egg, and ½ a pickled gherkin cut lengthwise. Roll up the slices and secure them with string.

Cut the onion into rings and fry the rings in margarine with a pinch of sugar until dark brown. Lay the olives on top, and sweat them for a few minutes. Add the garlic to the pan and enough simmering light ale to cover the olives but only just. Add a bayleaf, season with more salt and pepper, and cook slowly covered for about 1½ hours. Untie the string or cut it, lay the olives on a serving dish, remove the bayleaf and liquidize the gravy. Pour the gravy over the olives.

If the cooking pan doesn't look too dreadful (you are all men together), then don't bother to liquidize, munch the bay leaf, and serve straight from the pan.

All it needs is mashed potatoes or rice to accompany it.

Where are the olives? That's what you've made!

Serves 4–6

1½–2lb beef (4 slices from near rump)
2 Tablespoons French mustard
2 Tablespoons raw Easy Cook rice
1 hard-boiled egg
2 pickled gherkins
1 large onion
1 clove of garlic, crushed
½ pint light ale
1oz margarine
pinch sugar
1 bayleaf
salt, pepper

Cough, sneeze and gobble

It's arrived, the first cold of the autumn. So instead of going to a party in Chelsea, I am wearing an old shaggy dressing-gown, and sitting in front of an artificial coal fire. All I need is the ghost of Christmas Past and a nightcap, and I could be Scrooge.

I have surrounded myself with books on spirituality because when I begin to sneeze I start thinking of eternity. If your body lets you down it is natural, though not very super-natural, to turn to the soul as a replacement. I like reading books which I don't really understand, because in a fluey haze I sometimes think I do, which is the next best thing.

My temperature rises, and reason floats away. Perhaps I can find a backway into St Teresa's spiritual castle, and squat (spiritually) in one of her mansions. What would it be like lodging there? Need I pay VAT? Haziness descends again, and a light bulb fuses. I am befuddled and ask myself if this is a real Dark Night – or even darker? There is no answer to that one, and I sneeze again.

I turn to Dom Cuthbert Butler's *Western Mysticism* and decipher a paragraph on 'infused' and 'affective' contemplation. For some reason or other, this gives me great satisfaction, which is odd as I don't know what either term means. Perhaps it reminds me of my childhood and friar's balsam. Perhaps my grasshopper mind got 'illumined' or 'infused' without my knowing it. It is a tempting thought, but I am only just over 100 degrees F. so I can reject it.

Depression sets in, and I decide between coughs that I am just a low-grade spirit who will never ascend any Ladder of Perfection – just walk under it instead or around it more likely, knowing me. I won't have any visions like Julian of Norwich in her illness, only prattle on and on, like a Yiddish Margery Kempe. This strikes me as quite a humble thought and I cheer up sufficiently to go to the kitchen and get some food.

At the first sign of cold, I make myself a pot of stew. Neighbours and friends are caring in patches, and you are less resentful if you are self-sufficient. This is my favourite. It hails from the Mediterranean, and gets better with reheating.

The following recipe is substantial fare (cheap too) and it weighs me down to the material world. Even with a cough, I lick my lips and head for the casserole with a bowl in one hand, and a spoon in the other. Ambrosia and nectar will have to wait (if I am ever offered any, that is) and try meat, beans, and browned onions instead.

Am I confused or 'infused'? That's life.

Comfort casserole with meat and beans

Serves 1 several times
½lb haricot beans
2lb stewing steak, cubed
2 Tablespoons cooking oil
1½lb onions
¼lb smoked meat or sausage
1 Tablespoon flour
2 Tablespoons tomato purée
juice of ½ lemon
1–3 cloves garlic, crushed
1 wine glass red wine
½ teaspoon sugar
½ teaspoon dried thyme
salt, pepper

Soak the haricot beans overnight. Next day brown the cubed stewing steak in oil. Also cover the soaked beans with salted water and boil till tender – for about ¾ hour. Drain the beans, and reserve the liquid.

Slice the onions and fry them till golden with the chopped smoked meat. Add the flour. Stir in and make a roux with a mug of the bean liquid. When you have a thick sauce stir in the tomato purée, the lemon juice, garlic, red wine, sugar, and dried thyme. Salt and pepper. Bring to the boil stirring until the sauce bubbles.

Put the meat and cooked beans into a casserole. Pour the hot sauce over. Put the casserole in a pre-heated oven for about 2 hours (300°F Gas 2 150°C) till the meat is tender.

You can use cubed boned shoulder of lamb instead of stewing steak, and butter beans instead of haricot beans.

Spiritual technology

I should like to go back to America because I am fascinated by religious technology and ecclesiastical toys. I like banks of electric bulbs which light up (hopefully) when you put a coin in a slot.

In some places they are coloured sugar pink and duck-egg blue, so the effect is rather like a holy nursery.

I can sit for hours before machines which simulate clouds of violets and roses through which a saint appears to levitate with great detachment and without a hint of surprise.

In one place of worship they had substituted a tape for organ, choir and cantor. The effect was utterly insincere but quite enthralling.

I was also very taken by an Ecumenical Minister Doll. You could dress him up as a rabbi, or as a pastor, or as a Jesuit according to your religious fancy.

At first I nodded approvingly. This would make the kiddies fit for the pluralist interfaith and ecumenical society.

But then I hesitated. If they could turn a rabbi into a pastor before they could lisp might it not lure them into Relativism! Perhaps it would be better if they stuck to conkers and marbles, and left the 'educational toys' for theologians like me to play with, who have the necessary gravitas.

This easy savoury fish dish should be suitable for a rabbi, a pastor or a Jesuit as it contains no meat.

I am not so sure about Far Eastern co-religionists. People there do not eat milk products as we do, and one Thai friend told me once in an outburst of confidence, that to him most Western people smelt like corpses, because of all the dairy products they consumed.

They were addicted to cow, he said wonderingly.

Never-fail fish fillets

Serves 4

2lb cod or haddock fillets
½lb Lancashire cheese
1½ teaspoons English mustard
4 spring onions, chopped
1 whole tomato per fillet
cooking fat
salt, pepper

Grease a large oven-proof dish, and lay the fish fillets in it in one long row, skin side down. Grate the cheese (it is a good melter) and mix it with the mustard and chopped spring onions.

Spread the cheese mixture over the fish. Top with halved tomatoes, season, and put in a moderate oven (350°F Gas 4 180°C) for about half an hour. The top should be nicely browned.

I first ate this dish at my friend Pauline's. I have always liked it, because it doesn't go wrong, and I can be one of the fellas joining in the fun, even though I am cooking the meal.

My middle ages

I've turned 54, and decided it's a very nice age to be. I had always imagined life would get nastier as I grew older, but it hasn't been like that. To my surprise, my fifties are pleasanter than my forties or thirties, and I would never like to relive my teens and twenties again. Middle age brings a lot of unexpected bonuses and here are some I've discovered to my delight. I can now enjoy things on my own. I never used to. If I went to an art gallery, or on a holiday or a walk I had to tell somebody about my enjoyment before I could really enjoy it. I knew this was silly, but I couldn't do anything about it.

Now I find occasional doses of solitude increase my pleasure. I like sitting in a waiting-room or hotel lounge, just considering people, and trying to discern the souls that are deep within them. I like pottering around an empty house, opening a drawer here, taking out a book there, and nibbling any bits of chocolate I can find. I like being alone in a synagogue or church.

Another joy of middle age is that you have acquired the know-how about your own comfort. Over years of trial and error you have found out what you were told was true that scrambled eggs should be cooked slowly in a saucepan, not quickly in a frying-pan, and you know exactly the saucepan size for your own breakfast.

You have also learnt to position all the things you like around your easy chair – chocolate, spirituality, gramophone, telephone, toothpicks, poems, and pickled onions.

Yet another satisfaction is friends, true, tried and trusty friends, who know you through and through, who can look into you and through you and cackle over all your pomp, and pretensions, your little white lies (some not so little, but medium-size), your obstinacy, all the diets you never stuck to, all the good resolutions you don't keep, all the fickleness in you – and they remain friends.

There are other nice things too, and they balance the fact that your body isn't what it was, and is liable to let you down. In prayer for example, you don't agonize so much and so quickly. You give yourself time to settle down, arrange your prayer-books, and catch your breath. You aren't storming Heaven, just waiting patiently for the door to open and for you to walk in at a nice dignified trot, as befits the age of 54.

When you are middle-aged, you can get rid of that awful burden of expectation which you have had to carry since you were a child. If you like kippers with jam you can say so and do so (my mother does). If you want your cuppa in your goulash not with your goulash, why not?

This recipe for Goulash with a Cuppa was given to me by the film director Jan Kaplan. It has become a treat for me and some cronies of my generation. Why didn't we discover it at his age!

Jan Kaplan's goulash

Brown the meat cubes in hot oil then pour off the excess fat and keep the meat cubes warm. Sauté the onions (till light brown) and add the meat cubes, mixing them with half the paprika powder, the crushed garlic, cayenne pepper and some of the red sweet peppers.

Add to the mixture a little bit of the tea (just enough to prevent burning) and gently stew under a closed lid. Always keep checking the liquid level and adding small quantities of tea until the meat is almost cooked. Remove the lid and allow the liquid to evaporate (at this point let the meat go very dark brown). Sprinkle with flour then add the remaining tea, beef stock, glass of wine, remaining paprika and red peppers, sugar and marjoram to create a dark reddish brown spicy sauce. Half close the lid and gently stew till the meat is completely tender. Serve with boiled potatoes (boiled with 1 Tablespoon of carraway seeds) and sprinkle with freshly chopped parsley. Can be served with rice, noodles or bread (rye or 'black' continental).

Serves 6

2lb stewing beef, cut into bite-size cubes
2 Tablespoons vegetable oil
3 large onions, sliced
3 Tablespoons red paprika powder (again, Hungarian-produced is preferable)
1–2 teaspoons cayenne pepper (some like it hot)
2 red sweet peppers, cut into strips
2 cloves garlic
1 glass red wine (Hungarian 'Bull's Blood' or similar)
1 generous pint strong tea
¼ pint beef stock (beef stock cubes)
pinch marjoram
1 teaspoon sugar
parsley, finely chopped
salt and freshly milled pepper to taste
1 Tablespoon white flour

Variations:

So-called '*Znojemsky' goulash*': 3 or 4 pickled gherkins ('Krakus' or 'Nova' brand), finely chopped, are added to the cooked goulash or sprinkled over the finished dish.

Gipsy goulash: in the final stages of cooking add chopped and peeled tomatoes, two or three potatoes (cut into small pieces). Fried, thinly cut rings of onion are sprinkled over the dish (gipsy music in the background is optional).

Livers and lovers

An African friend of mine told me his great aunt had a factory in the bush for making love potions. The recipes were very secret, and handed down in the family, like those of the higher-class bottled sauces you find in expensive grocers, or the classy liqueurs brewed by contemplatives, whose price you dare not contemplate.

Her ingredients showed enterprise and daring, and a sort of jungle chic. All the best cook books tell you to be imaginative with offal, and that she certainly was. The strangest organs and appendices mixed with liver and lights were pounded together, raising hell in the emotional life of the very young and the very old, who were her clientèle.

Her methods were less sophisticated than her ingredients, and involved mortars, pestles, grinding rocks and bashing. A food processor or a simple blender would have been invaluable, but where could she have plugged it in, and who could sell her an adaptor?

A lady friend of mine asked me for advice. She had been 'walking out' with her young man for many years, though he was not so young, and her age was so certain as to be speculative. She wanted to stimulate him into a proposal. She would set the scene with a comfy dinner, and she swore a mighty oath that neither would rise from the table until he had popped the question.

What should she serve? Garlic had strange properties – too strange perhaps, and unpredictable. Caviare was out also; they would soon need a deposit on a mortgage.

I suggested Italian liver. All men like it served with fluffy mash. It also goes well with heavy red wine, and would put him in a good temper. It wasn't a love potion, but satisfying, nonetheless.

Slice the onion into rings, and slice into fine strips the tender liver. (If it wasn't that tender in the first place, marinate it for a few hours before, then dry.) Melt the fat and olive oil in a pan. Cook the onions very slowly until soft. Toss the liver strips in flour seasoned with salt and pepper and add to the onions. Stir until the liver is just cooked. Season, and add the vermouth or Marsala and cook for a minute more. Sprinkle with fresh parsley. That's all.

Serves 2
¾lb calves' or lambs' liver or ox (if marinated in wine, with herbs, seasoning and 1 Tablespoon olive oil)
1 large onion
2 Tablespoons fat
4 Tablespoons olive oil
2 Tablespoons sweet vermouth or Marsala
flour, pepper, salt
fresh parsley

And what happened, you may ask? Well, drowsy with liver, lights, and wine, he mumbled some words contentedly. These words she assured him later were the clearest possible proposal she had ever heard. She accepted naturally, and pinned a note on his woolly to remind him. They are very happy. Perhaps there is something about offal after all.

How I cope with my paper God

There is a streak of harmless meanness in most of us and as we get older I think it intensifies. It ceases to have anything to do with economy and becomes a pure passion like that of a collector of first editions, or like that of boys who write down train numbers with unrewarded devotion.

My father, for example, was born before the Health Service doled out pills to the worthy and unworthy alike. It grieved my father to see a capsule or a tablet lying forgotten on the washstand. He regularly went round the house and put all the remnants in a plastic bottle in the medicine chest. I raided the plastic bottle for years thinking I was taking Aspirin. So did my mother. We discovered this 'economy' some months after he died. It is odd, all things considered, that we survived and he went first.

A friend of mine will not throw away remnants of cooked food. She starved during the war, so she is forgiven, but I am dubious about dining with her.

If the blackened sprig of cauliflower was turned down the first time, then a week's burial in foil in the depths of the fridge is not going to make it more palatable.

'Age', as Shakespeare said, could not 'stale the infinite variety' of Cleopatra, but it certainly stales stale veg.

My own hoarding problem is a curious one. My grandfather, out of piety or superstition or both, had instructed me never to throw away any bit of paper on which was written the name of 'God' in any of its forms, or indeed in any language.

Now in my papers this word occurs often (this is not name-dropping, just a professional hazard), and my drawers accumulate worn-out prayer-books, scraps of notes, letters from pious friends, and holy texts on bookmarks. I just can't bring myself to throw them in the dustbin, but I have no means to bury this holy débris in a consecrated cemetery either, which is the traditional Jewish way of getting rid of such things. Cemetery space is as expensive now as living space in a chic suburb.

One meanness of which I do not approve, is pouring the little bits of wine left in the bottom of bottles into a decanter and serving it with dinner to trusting guests. The lees of red wine may be a cause of migraine, and the alcohol content is so unpredictable that anything could happen to even a moderate drinker.

There is one magic way of dealing with scraps of cooked meat or veg. and it is called Risotto. Provided you don't get too mean, and the mixture is not too bizarre the result can be more than 'interesting'. Here is my version.

Risotto

Chop the following raw items and fry in the margarine in a saucepan: the onion, garlic, celery and green pepper (if you have them) and any bits of smoked meat.

Wash a cup of rice in a colander, shake it dry and add it to the pan. Stir the rice but don't bash it. As the round Italian rice absorbs liquid, fry the rice for 2 or 3 minutes, and then add the first cup of hot bouillon (made with cubes but make it stronger than usual). Let it simmer slowly.

When the bouillon has been absorbed add all the *cooked* bits — chicken, scraps of meat, salami bits, mushrooms, peas or runner-beans, together with the second cup of hot bouillon and fresh herbs. You may have to add more bouillon before the rice is cooked.

Continue to simmer until the rice is soft and all the bouillon is absorbed. You can be as imaginative as you like with additions provided the result is tasty and colourful. (I substitute, for example, smoked fish for meat whenever I want to add grated cheese.) Salt and pepper.

When it is done, adjust for salt and pepper, stir in a lump of margarine and sprinkle with

Serves 4
1 large onion
1–2 cloves garlic
1 piece celery
1 green pepper
any smoked meat (bacon for you, beef for me)
fresh herbs
1 cup round Italian rice
2oz good margarine
2 cups hot bouillon
cooked meat and vegetable leftovers
grated Cheddar cheese (with this Jews use smoked fish not meat)
salt, pepper
chopped parsley

grated Cheddar and chopped
parsley. Don't use the Cheddar too
fresh. Serve hot with green salad.

Reheated meat must be cooked
through thoroughly not just
warmed. I am cautious about using
recooked meat or fish which has
once been frozen.

I am never sure how irrational these hoarding habits are. Do they
have any basis in reality?

I know that I can throw away without a qualm pieces of paper on
which I have coyly and cunningly replaced the 'o' in 'God' with a
dash. But when I have been foolish enough to leave the vowel, I
dither and hoard it in my desk drawer.

I wonder what the Almighty makes of the extraordinary be-
haviour of His creatures. Did He think we would really turn out like
this?

'Goose on the dole'

Some read cookery books to provide food for their body, and others to
provide food for thought. I like reading the second type before I go to
sleep. I can get the comfort of 'comfort eating' without actually
eating.

It's becoming difficult to find novels or stories with a happy ending,
and cookery books of the romantic type do just that.

I like them with pictures, when you see a clean smiling cook ('has
she seen a vision?') looking compassionately at you over a Bavaroise
or Glazed Goose, both decorated with twirls, turrets, and cherries,
and the goose dressed up in frilly paper pants (the final indignity!).

There are no flies on her – the cook, not the goose. Her pinny is
spotless and starched, and though she is holding a chopping knife,
there is no tell-tale plaster on her manicured fingers. Around her are
the tools of her craft, prettily arranged on a carved oak kitchen table.

She is a homely creature, just like you and me. There is her mortar
and pestle, her bottle of virgin olive oil (first pressing), and her basil
pot. She doesn't use mixed herbs.

I dream about her sometimes. Together we peel without tears symmetrical little onions for Boeuf Bourguignon, we blow the air into profiteroles and she glazes her gammon. (I can't accompany her because of the Jewish food laws.) She looks as if she might get tetchy, if you didn't lard your joint.

Morning comes, and reality with it. You search around in all your old jacket pockets, and find you've got in small coins nearly £3. You also have an old half-crown, and eight Greek drachmas (value unknown). You have to provide dinner for six on it. It's no use going to her with her basil pot. She wasn't meant for the likes of you and me.

Go back instead to the recipes of childhood, to depression dumplings and austerity feasts. They were often surprisingly good. Goose on the dole is my answer to her glazed wonder.

Mock goose (Liver hotpot)

Soak the liver for several hours in water with 2 teaspoons of vinegar. This helps to get rid of the over-strong taste. Rinse it and dry it. Drain the liver slices and dip them in seasoned flour.

Mix together the chopped onion, apple, garlic, sage and smoked meat.

In a casserole thickly greased with margarine or dripping put in a layer of liver. On top of that put a layer of the onion, apple and smoked meat mixture. Salt and pepper. Repeat the layers. On top put a thick layer of thinly sliced potatoes. Dot it with dripping or margarine. Salt and pepper again.

Mix some hot water with the Marmite and Worcester sauce. Pour it into the casserole but leave the top potato layer well above the plimsoll line as you want it to brown.

Serves 4

1½lb ox liver, thinly sliced
2 teaspoons vinegar
2lb potatoes, peeled and
    thinly sliced
2 medium onions, chopped
2 dessert apples, chopped
1 clove of garlic, chopped
1 teaspoon dried sage
¼lb smoked meat (I use
    smoked sausage), chopped
flour
dripping or margarine
2 teaspoons salt
½ teaspoon pepper
½ teaspoon Marmite
1 Tablespoon Worcester
    sauce

Cook the casserole for 1 hour covered, in the top of the oven (325°F Gas 3 160°C) and then remove the cover for a further ½ hour. Raw potatoes take longer to cook in an oven than you think.

All the ingredients amalgamate, the top is crisp, and the liver is very tender. The version above is a kosher one. Otherwise you could use milk instead of the water and vinegar, and bacon instead of smoked sausage or beef.

Goose on the dole is not a romantic dish, just a delicious one. Yet for me there is a whiff of nostalgia about it.

N.B. This recipe was known as Goose on the dole, because it was supposed to taste like goose. It doesn't!

Exotic but not expensive

My friend Pauline gives kitchen suppers. We sit comfortably in old shabby elegant chairs round a scrubbed table, while Pauline cooks in front of us, thinking aloud as she does so.

'Shall I add an anchovy to the tomato salad?' she mutters, or 'I bet I could make a quiche out of that courgette,' or 'Let's have that too, why not?'

As Pauline muses, and the food gets more and more delicious, I bless God for all the cooks who say: 'Why not?' rather than 'Why?' which is such a mean question.

And all around us bubbles come out of strange containers like mediaeval alchemy or modern science fiction. Air escapes from little glass locks on the fermenting jars standing on the fridge, on the dresser and on the kitchen shelves, and it seems that the kitchen itself has its own life and is breathing deeply and gravely and comfortably, as a wholesome friendly kitchen should breathe.

Gradually the tensions of the office dissolve. My muscles relax. I look at the bits of china on the table – all good, none matching, each a triumph tracked down in junk shops and street markets.

I too start to breathe gravely and comfortably in time to the fermenting jars.

I look at the kitchen tools, and the saucepans and the fish kettle, all immaculate and warm, a little dented, and just right for their job, and I feel a sense of satisfaction, of the sheer rightness of things.

It is like a domestic *Te Deum* or a kitchen Canticle.

Pauline looks up, and glances at me. 'Would I like a glass of her wheat wine?' she asks, or meditatively, 'perhaps a glass of parsnip, or why not open that bottle of parsley champagne. We could all do with a little sparkle,' she exclaims. 'Why not!'

So the parsley is opened with a pop, and a sparkle starts up within us, and we become rather witty, and our conversation sparkles – at least it seems to. There is more to parsley than meets the eye.

While we are sparkling, Pauline prepares these kidneys.

Pauline's kidneys provençales

Very gently sauté the kidneys for about 10 minutes in the margarine and 1 tablespoon of oil. Remove the kidneys from the pan and leave to drain on kitchen paper. Save the remaining juices from the pan.

Sauté the sliced onions gently in the rest of the oil with the garlic until they become transparent and soft.

Add the chopped green pepper and continue cooking until it too becomes soft.

Now add to the pan the can of tomatoes, the tomato purée, red wine, sugar and 2 or 3 pinches of thyme. Leave this mixture to continue to cook slowly for at least 15 minutes. It will thicken and reduce and when this has happened you can add salt and pepper to taste.

Slice the kidneys into 6 or 8

Serves 4
6 lamb's kidneys
2 medium onions
8oz tin tomatoes (pulped)
1½ Tablespoons tomato
    purée
1 small sweet green pepper
1oz margarine
3 Tablespoons cooking oil
1 clove garlic, chopped
thyme
1 teaspoon sugar
1 glass red wine
salt, pepper

according to size. Add these and
their juices to the sauce and allow
to cook for about 10 minutes,
stirring them from time to time
until the kidneys are finally cooked
but still pink and tender.

Serve on a bed of rice and
sprinkled with chopped parsley.

The hot potato adventure

To my surprise I have been invited to America to lecture on religion
in Europe. Though I am fond of Europe, is its religion at the moment
notable for its quantity or its quality? Will a certain amount of
'cooking' be required to justify my journey? Still we may possess
treasures of sanctity in ourselves, we are just too modest to recognize.

A good reason for going is another type of cooking, generous and
American.

Unlike many other Europeans, I enjoy American food. The break-
fasts are sheer delight with waffles, sausages, and maple syrup, and
an American sandwich garnished with coleslaw makes an English
sandwich seem shameful and mean, with its blotting-paper bread,
smeared not covered with margarine, and a fraud of a filling.

I also enjoy American wine. The Christian Brothers produce some
in California, which would bring credit to France.

Upper State New York, unlikely as it seems, is also a good source of
cheap and excellent quality wine.

I also think if you are going to drink plain water, it's better to ice it
American style, and anaesthetize your taste-buds.

The restaurants, too, can be tasteful in many ways. One I patro-
nized was in the shape of a pineapple, four storeys high, and another
had a front like a great Cheddar cheese. This exuberance either
stimulates your juices or takes away appetite for ever. I can only
applaud, and order another double-decker on rye with a chocolate
malted.

Americans are ingenious about simple foods. Take a baked potato
for example – or better take two, for they are addictive. In Britain

and Ireland, they are adorned discreetly with butter, salt and pepper and that's it. Americans have more adventure.

American hot potatoes

Wash, scrub, and grease the potatoes, and bake them in a hot oven. Make a small cut in their tops. Don't spoil them by wrapping them in foil. They take about an hour.

Now cut them in two, and scoop out some of their innards. Mix them quickly with the sour cream, chopped green spring onions or chives, and salt and pepper.

Put the mixture back. Do so quickly because the potatoes should be eaten hot.

For another filling, fry a chopped onion and pimento, add chopped corned beef, and when it is piping hot, stuff the potatoes.

If you don't mind packets, make up a thick cheese sauce (you can add some of your own cheese grated to pep it up). Into it stir cooked peas and mushrooms, and a drop of cooking sherry. Stuff the potatoes, sprinkle with more cheese and paprika, and heat quickly under a hot grill.

Mashed tuna is good with mayonnaise, and I enjoy an unlikely stuffing of tinned mackerel mashed with some curry powder, mango chutney and mayonnaise.

So is cream cheese, mixed with chopped raw onions and grated cheddar.

Serves 4

4 large floury potatoes (never use new)

½ pint sour cream
1 bunch spring onions or chives
salt, pepper
or
1 large onion, chopped
1 pimento
½lb corned beef, chopped
or
cheese sauce (from a packet)
4oz peas
4oz mushrooms
1 dessert spoon cooking sherry
grated cheese, paprika
or
small tin tuna
1 Tablespoon mayonnaise
or
1 small tin mackerel
1 teaspoon curry powder
1 teaspoon mango chutney
1 Tablespoon mayonnaise
or
4oz cream cheese
1 medium raw onion
2oz Cheddar cheese

Never, never throw away the skins – that's the nicest part. Crisped up in the oven, sprinkled with salt and some oil, they are delicious as cocktail snacks and are a sort of vegetarian crackling. They are much nicer than bought crisps.

Not only fit for a dog

I never intended to buy my dog Re'ach. I was actually going to buy some cat food, but while I was waiting, I had to pass a cage of puppies. Unwisely, I started to play with one little mite through the cage with a finger.

I got my cat food, but as I left the shop a yearning, reproachful look followed me up the street. I didn't want a dog. I had to take services and visit hospitals. What would I do with the tiny mite while I was sitting on an ecclesiastical committee? ('Would Your Grace kindly pass my dog a bone?'). Could I take her to a funeral? Good Lord, anything might happen!

I rushed back to the shop and bought her, for it was love at first sight (the only time it has ever happened to me).

I took her to the vet. immediately. 'What have you got there?' he asked.

'I don't really know,' I answered, looking proud and besotted, 'but I think he is a small terrier'.

'Terrier,' he snorted, 'look at the paws! I'd say it was a cross between an Alsatian and a Labrador.' (And so it was.) 'As for male – well, God forgive you – it's all the sense you can ever get from a minister of religion.'

She (not he) was in fact very big, very sentimental, and very obstinate. (Where did she get those qualities from?) She was also quite pious.

I took her to services. When the congregation stood she stood, and when they sat she sat. She even gave a whoof after my sermon when the choir sang Amen.

Sometimes when I came back late, there was no time to shop and Re'ach and I used to eat whatever we could find in the house.

There was usually some spaghetti, eggs and cheese. This is what we made, and it is in fact a simple and classical Italian dish. As both of us only ate once a day, the portions we cooked were ample.

Cook the spaghetti in lots of boiling salted water. Drain it through a sieve which fits into the top of another saucepan. (The spaghetti will keep warm over the water in the saucepan, which you leave to simmer and steam.)

While all this is going on, beat together 3 whole eggs, 3 egg yolks, a ½ cup of grated cheese, the cream and some grinds of pepper. Stir all this into the spaghetti while it is still hot.

The heat from the spaghetti will cook the egg mixture just enough. The amount of salt you use will depend on the cheese. (It should be Parmesan, but was usually strong Cheddar.)

If you are a Christian, you can add little strips of bacon fried in their own fat. If you are Moslem use smoked beef. If you are Jewish, hard cheese!

Serves 2 ministers and 4 terriers
1lb spaghetti
6 eggs
4oz grated cheese
3 Tablespoons cream
salt, black pepper
Parmesan cheese or Cheddar
**Flavouring as dictated by
    faith**

70

Re'ach lived to over 18 years, but since she died I don't seem to make this very often. But you can. It was fit for a mongrel and me.

My retreat is the kitchen

The Day of Atonement has gone, with its long and repetitive prayers, and I am pooped.

As a child I used to repeat one word over and over again, quicker and quicker, and to my delight it turned into nonsense. It's like that even with religion. You have said the same things so many times that there is no freshness in the words, and life has drained away from them.

Then it is time to retreat and let yourself be surprised by God. Some go to the country and others to a retreat house for that surprise.

I don't do either. I retreat to a kitchen in Holland and sit in the corner, letting the committees drift out of my mind, with their points of order and lectures on 'Whither Theology?' or is it 'Wither Theology!' – in that state, you get muddled – and the 'in-five-minutes-you're-on-Rabbi' sermons.

As they drift away, I decide to forget about religion and just be conscious of the ordinary world around me.

I sniff the cinnamon as Anneke assembles a deep and generous Dutch apple pie. Her husband, Aad, is chopping wood for the stove, and the wood smell mingles with the cinnamon, deepening and enriching it.

On the table are all the lovely things Dutch people put on bread and butter. There are pink and white aniseed balls known as little mice, dark molasses made from apple-peel, slices of 'nail' cheese (the nails are cloves which give the cheese its flavour), and somewhere there is the faintest promise in the air of Dutch herring, the tastiest treat on earth.

And as I sniff I take in too the kindness of my friends who provide them for me so freely. And then I realize that He too is there, showing himself in their kindness. So sitting in the kitchen corner, I say the first fresh prayer I've uttered for weeks: 'Thank you.'

Tonight we are going to eat a Bohemian Hunters' Dish. This is my adaptation.

71

Overnight soak the prunes in tea. Drain them next morning and store.

Fry the sliced onion, garlic and smoked meat in a little fat until the onion is soft.

Roll stewing steak cubes in seasoned flour and add to the pan.

Let the meat brown. Then add just enough brown ale to barely cover, the sage, bay leaf, French mustard and Worcester sauce.

Simmer gently for 1½ hours, stirring every so often to make sure nothing is sticking to the bottom. Add the prunes and whole mushrooms and cook for a further 30 minutes.

When this is done, adjust the seasoning and pour the contents into a broad shallow dish. Make sure it is not awash with gravy. Cover with a thick layer of seasoned mashed potatoes, dot with fat and a sprinkle of paprika, and pop into a hot oven.

When the top is brown, serve it with a green vegetable.

It is so good you will say another prayer, not a liturgical prayer but a kitchen prayer, spontaneous, sincere and straight from the tummy!

Serves 6
8 prunes
½ pint of tea (China or Earl Grey are best, but any type that Bohemian hunters drink will do)
2oz cooking fat
1 medium onion, sliced
1 clove garlic, chopped
¼lb smoked meat
1½lb stewing steak, cut into 1 inch cubes
½–1 pint brown ale
½lb mushrooms
½ teaspoon sage
1 bay leaf
1 teaspoon French mustard
1 teaspoon Worcester sauce
2lb potatoes, boiled and mashed
flour
salt, pepper, paprika to taste

A *time to shed tears*

The Bible says that you should love your neighbour as yourself. All the religious people I know genuinely try to love their neighbour. They try so hard that it hurts. What they often forget is the last two words of the text. They don't love themselves. Not many people can take pity on others if they don't keep some charity for themselves too.

The more I listen to people in my office, the more I realize what a tough proposition a human life is – always trying to join together spirit and matter, conscience and the instincts, the needs of others and sheer self-survival.

Not long ago at a dinner party someone I know burst into tears. It was just too much! There are periods in your life when the tears just have to come out. It's nothing to be ashamed of, it's a very good thing in fact. The pains and the sorrows have come to the surface and to light. Then they are no longer buried and festering away behind our party face.

At such periods it can be a wise move to find a trained counsellor, partly because we don't have the detachment to see ourselves, partly because we don't have enough compassion or kindness for ourselves.

People sometimes add to the genuine crosses God gives them to bear some rather fiendish ones of their own devising. It isn't always easy to sort them out.

I know some rabbis, priests and nuns who have been trained as counsellors. The combination can be tremendous and very helpful to people like me who are negotiating their way through the shallows and rapids of middle age.

A Chinese philosopher once said that you should exercise the same care and consideration for yourself and others, as you would when making an omelette. I can't give an omelette recipe because I can't make one, a proper one that is. I don't have that easy touch which comes when you are at home with yourself.

But I do know a number of ways of cooking peasant omelettes which cause no anxiety and no tears.

Soak the sheets of Matzo in hot water (see 'Re-living the Exodus' on p. 135). Squeeze, drain, and crumble. Stir in the beaten eggs with a pinch of salt. Heat the oil in a frying-pan and pour in the mixture. When it is set put the pan under a hot grill to brown the top. Scatter liberally with sugar and a dusting of cinnamon and serve.

For a savoury omelette, carefully wash a leek and cut it into ¼-inch slices. Fry them in the oil until they are soft and browning. Pour the beaten eggs over them salted and peppered, and finish as above.

An even nicer addition are chunks of spring onion instead of leeks. Stir these into the eggs, before pouring into the pan. I have also eaten a good peasant omelette which had as a filling croutons of bread fried with garlic and parsley.

Eggs can also be mixed successfully with a small tin of Baby Spinach purée and chopped walnuts. Make sure the spinach liquid is poured away. The green omelette looks pretty.

Serves 2
3 sheets Matzo
4 eggs, beaten
2 Tablespoons oil
sugar, cinnamon, salt to taste
or
4 eggs, beaten
1 leek or 4 spring onions
3 Tablespoons oil
pepper, salt
Alternative fillings:
croutons, garlic, parsley
or
spinach purée, chopped walnuts
or
smoked salmon, cream

SHARING VEGETABLES WITH VEGETARIANS AND OTHERS

Some years ago I went on a holiday to Portugal. The food was good and on New Year's Eve the chef made a special effort. He arranged a buffet table glowing with roasts, salads, platters, fruits, and trifles. In the centre was a whole lamb skinned and roasted. In its right eye was a winking red light and in its left a winking green one. I have always liked lambs. I have played with them in fields, and was very fond of Larry the Lamb on BBC children's radio. For six years after that I became a vegetarian, and one day I shall be one again, because though I like the taste of meat I have never been comfortable about the slaughter of it, whatever the form. Also battery farming is a constant worry. Being a town person I am squeamish about the crude facts of life.

Vegetarianism has become easier because the soya substitutes have become less nasty, and occasionally enjoyable. Also in many vegetarian restaurants you consume good food, not bad ideology, and can get wine and a chair with a back to it. Another advantage of vegetarianism is that I can entertain people of different faiths, and even of my own faith, without finding out what they can eat and what they can't. As they are often not quite honest with themselves about such matters let alone honest with me, I need the patience of a Maigret with the intuition of Miss Marple to work out a suitable menu.

I began to waver in my vegetarianism partly because I was the only vegetarian in the household, and I had troubles enough without arguments about ox liver and nuts.

If you are that way inclined yourself, then good luck and I hope this section helps you.

Where is the Beef? (Advice in Lent)

There is a puritan streak in me which compels me to enter Health Shops, Food Reform Shops, and Pure Food Shops.

They are pleasant places, cleaner and quieter than the carnivorous supermarkets, and I like browsing round them, as being a townsman I do not want to see bleeding lumps of flesh or chicken corpses.

I am an on-and-off sort of semi-vegetarian. On, because the Jewish food laws make meat difficult, and off because I am the only 'sort of' vegetarian in the family and it causes chaos.

I also like low things such as liver and lights, so I am making no claim to virtue, and you should not therefore feel over-trumped in purity by such an inconsistent person as me.

I like all the odd things you can find in health shops. Herbal cigarettes are prettily packed, and even more prettily priced. I tried the menthol and the honey varieties on the several occasions I stopped smoking. They were comforting but disconcerting as there was no lift from the nicotine. The scent was strong too. I enjoyed it but my secretary didn't until she got hooked on the honey variety as well.

The meat substitutes raise an interesting problem. If they are not meat but taste like meat, then are they permissible say in Lent or according to the Jewish food laws? That's an interesting moral point.

In the past I used to avoid them all, because I didn't like the soya aftertaste. But in recent years they have got much better.

I was given at a dinner some knitted pseudo-chicken. It tasted bland but wholesome and I was as delighted as a child to find it came with a plastic wish-bone! Alas – the maker's name was not woven in.

Some mixes taste (I am told) uncommonly like pre-war piggy bangers. They satisfy meat eaters, and a packet on the shelf keeps a long time.

If you want to tart it up for a dinner party, you can use this *roulade*, which I invented on the spur of the moment when some important people dropped in for a meal. I made a Swiss roll out of it, layering it with spinach and onion sauce, and then baked it.

It was good hot, but I am not so keen on any of the meat substitutes when cold. Another good one is Burgamix, which makes a pleasant sort of hamburger when hot and accompanied by the normal garnishes, and a thick slice of raw onion.

There is also a surprisingly good imitation of chicken fat which is purely vegetarian. I got a pot at Selfridge's and I marvelled. If you should want a vegetarian chicken fat, then I recommend it, and it is called Mazchik. Chicken fat in Jewish households plays the same role as dripping in gentile ones.

Perhaps you can afford a Ginseng root, and after munching it, virtue will be its own reward, you may look 20 years younger!

This is an easy recipe for a vegi 'Schnitzel Holstein'! If you persevere you become addicted to the smoky taste of aubergine. It is a great replacer of meat.

Aubergine schnitzel

Serves 2–3
1 long aubergine
1 egg, beaten
bread crumbs or matzo meal
plain flour
salt, pepper
cooking oil
2–3 eggs, poached or fried

Wash the aubergine and cut off the ends. Slice it lengthways in ½-inch slices. Use at least 1 slice per person. Dip the slices in seasoned flour, 1 beaten egg and bread crumbs, or matzo meal (cracker crumbs are a good substitute). Fry the aubergine slices until they are tender in deep oil. Drain and serve them with a poached or fried egg on top.

They taste a bit like steak, if you use your imagination.

All's fare in the railway war

I have decided to stop sighing over British Rail and am going to enjoy it instead. After all many things are tragic or comic according to the attitude you bring to them. In the past, I used to like such games as bridge or Mastermind, but I have given them up in favour of the railway tariff. It's a battle of wits between me and them over the fares. You know the sort of thing you face, as you go to buy your ticket: if you are a cripple aged between 55 and 60, travelling to X on Tuesday afternoons between 11.55 a.m. and 2.35 p.m. and returning via Y on the 13th of the following month, you get a reduction of 11½ per cent on the full fare (reduced to 10½ per cent if the 13th is a

Friday). If you take up the business as a hobby, you can make the most extraordinary journeys (£1 supplement, first class) quite cheaply. Of course, it's not where you want to go but that is beside the point.

Another thing I like on the train is the licence to peer into other people's gardens and backyards. I have always liked gnomes with fishing rods, perched on mushrooms, and the only reason I haven't got one myself is that gnomes come expensive these days. I have had to be content with two concrete remaindered rabbits.

There is one back garden in the Midlands densely populated with polystyrene gnomes and plastic elves, and I am so filled with admiration that I have toyed with the idea of getting off the train and dallying.

But dallying would, of course, invalidate my Special Super Duper Inter-Village Saver, and I would have to pay 6¾ per cent excess on £2.91½p. I prefer to translate another medieval Hebrew document than work that one out for I am a pre-computer.

Another joy is the buffet car. I mean it seriously. One great expert on food said a great delight of British cooking is the railway pork pie. I, of course, cannot confirm or deny this but their fruit cake has enough cherries (I counted them). Also, there is a nice line in backchat in the queue, provided you are not standing on the join between two carriages.

A train journey is also a good time for spiritual reading. There is no telephone (yet), and people are usually very polite.

Life is also a journey, and it is pleasant to remember that while you are travelling home, you are also travelling to your eternal home (though you don't want to get there too fast).

For railway eating, I suggest Greek pitta bread. You can buy them in packets, and if you slice off the top you have a very convenient bread pocket to put things in, much easier to munch than a conventional sandwich, where the filling can spill out.

Pitta and Felafel

At the same kind of shop where you buy pitta you will also get Felafel mix. It comes from the Middle East and is made of ground spiced chick-peas. Reconstitute it according to the packet directions (I add an extra clove of garlic, and a minced deseeded green chili). Roll it into little balls and fry them in hot oil till brown all over.

Fill the pittas with Felafel balls, cut up pickled cucumber, hard-boiled egg, cooked or tinned pimento, and tomato slices. Salt and pepper the mixture.

On a less adventurous level, scrambled eggs, and left over Ratatouille make a pleasant filling. They are very convenient and very sustaining.

The chick-peas contain a lot of protein. With a vacuum flask of hot tea or chilled white wine with soda water and a dash of Ribena, you are not bothered by the vagaries of the Buffet Car.

Bits and pieces

One of the greatest difficulties of life and cookery is to know what to do with bits. There is a magpie in all of us, and until we decide to disgorge, there is enough tucked away in our cupboards to supply church bazaars, tombolas and countless bring-and-buys. Some people I know get so addicted to knick-knackerie that half of their life is spent in acquiring chipped plates and souvenirs from the seaside, and they fill in the rest of their time with trundling their loot to the nearest charity shop.

There, of course, they are tempted again (that old magpie), and before they can get out of the door they have bought another basket of bargains.

Now some things really are worth getting. Provided you don't care if they don't match, it is still possible to pick up some lovely china plates and saucers.

I think a dinner table can look lovely with good-quality oddments. All the remnants of Royal Worcester, Minton and Spode make a jewelled effect like a Persian carpet. People peer at each other's plates to see what treasures they have been dealt. I don't think an occasional chip matters – most of us are, after all, a bit chipped anyway.

I also like second-hand cooking pans, kitchen tools and casseroles. They are usually heavier and better than what is offered nowadays. I have a treasured fish kettle which cost 10p and a cauldron which looks grim and medieval but is terrific for spaghetti.

I also found an old sampler, a bit 'mothy', but still readable. It was worked by a girl named Phoebe Lawson in 1800. She went to Ackworth School and she had embroidered these words on it.

'One of the most illustrious but at the same Time one of the most difficult of the Christian Duties is to love our Enemies and to pray for the Welfare and Amendment of them who do spitefully use and persecute us.'

I have always been touched by this Christian voice from the past. It would have surprised her to know the effect of her words on a middle-aged rabbi nearly two centuries after she laid it aside.

To us the ways of God often seem accidental, but they are providential.

Anyway, I hope she got a prize for it because the letters are most conscientiously done even if her 'a's are a little wobbly.

Some of the best dishes I know have been made with bits and pieces. Some novices I knew used to make a dish called 'Curried Rubbish' at the end of each week. It had bits of pilchard in it, and parsnips and cold porridge, and remnants of rice pudding. They let it cook slowly in a great pan on an Aga cooker. At their priory we ate in silence, so I could never ask for more; I just prayed and it was granted – two or three times in fact.

This simple dish came to me by a circuitous route from Baroness Vera von der Heydt, a great psycho-analyst, a very great lady, and author of *Prospects for the Soul*, which I recommend to all religious. You can use in it your leftover raw and cooked vegetables (tomatoes, mushrooms, carrots, aubergines etc.).

Baroness semolina with cheese and vegetables

Serves 4 as accompaniment; 2/3 as main dish

1 pint milk
5 Tablespoons semolina
½ teaspoon mustard (dry or prepared)
1 teaspoon mixed herbs
4oz grated cheese
2oz butter
vegetables (cooked and leftover)
salt, pepper

Warm the milk with the herbs and flavourings. Before it boils add the semolina. Stir constantly on a low heat until it thickens. Pour it into a plate and let it cool completely. Cut it into squares. Put them into a greased oven-proof dish with layers of grated cheese, small pieces of butter and the cooked vegetables. Finish with a layer of cheese. Bake in a moderate oven (350°F Gas 4 180°C) for about 20–25 minutes.

For big portions (prayer makes you hungry, and silent prayer even more so), double the quantities.

I like reading French cookery books, though they always make me feel such a slob. They are so exact, so precise, and so perfectionist. There is no nonsense about 'making do', or pretending the liver of some tired old ox will taste like goose.

Good food, they say, needs good ingredients, and that means money and time and care. So, when French books say turnips, they mean *navets*, not great white lumps, but little delicate white globes, and when they say cream, they do not mean top of the milk – not even gold top at that.

You also have to take the measurements seriously, and start counting your *décis*.

A girl I know went to Paris to work. 'My!' she exclaimed when we met. 'I thought I dressed quite well in England, but in Paris I have to take twice as long. Everything has to fit exactly, and be just right. It has to match and not just "go with". I never realized quite how comfortable and sloppy we were back home.'

It's the same with French spirituality. I have just been reading *The Story of a Soul* by St Thérèse of Lisieux, and underneath all the little flowers and Victorian débris there is the same exactness and precision and perfectionism. Like the French cookery books, I once again feel such a slob with my vague stabs at spirituality.

I shan't ever become a French cook. I am not built that way. I shall always 'make do', 'go with' and 'get by'. I shall make my Boeuf Bourguignon with sliced onions, not with peeled shallots, because they are so much easier. I shall sneak in chuck steak though the recipe requires rump, because it is cheaper. I shall use whole eggs, not yolks for my mayonnaise, because I know I'll forget about all those whites solidifying in the fridge.

I shall never become a 'little flower' like St Thérèse either. It will always be one and a half steps forwards, and one and three-eighths steps backwards.

Please God, He will 'make do' with me, and I'll 'get by' at the judgment. Is there a patron saint for slobs, I wonder?

This dish comes from the Dauphiné, near Grenoble and it is easy to make and not expensive, even if you do use real butter and cream, not just marge and the top of the milk. It deserves good treatment.

Gratin dauphinois

Peel the potatoes and slice very thinly. Squeeze out excess liquids with a clean tea towel. Crush the garlic into the butter. Mix. Use half of it to butter a flat oven-proof dish. Lay in it a layer of potatoes. Salt and add 2 to 3 tablespoons of cream. Carry on doing this until all the potatoes are used up. Pour the remaining cream in, add a little butter, and grated cheese. Cook for about 1¼ hours at 325°F Gas 3 160°C.

Serves 6
2lb potatoes (I use King Edwards)
½ pint whipping cream or more if preferred
1 clove garlic
2oz butter
4oz grated Gruyère or Emmental
1½ teaspoons of salt
nutmeg

Food for the poor

My grandparents were poor, really poor. My parents were lower middle class, hanging on by the skin of their teeth. I think it is easier to be poor, really poor, than insecure middle class. You don't get so battered spiritually.

If you are poor, for example, you are free from social pretensions. You may have to pretend to the neighbours, but you don't pretend to yourself. When you touch bottom it is too real for illusion or false reassurance.

I think poverty can be endured and even enjoyed if you can share it. Some people (like me) need other people to share it with, and joke about it. Others, more fortunate, can share their poverty with God.

When you are poor, you become ingenious. You get a nose for a bargain, and you experiment. You become original, and some of the best dishes in the world are the fruit of poverty. You search through cookery books trying to find out how to make scraps delectable, and how far you can stretch a slice of beef before it becomes transparent.

The food of poverty in Eastern Europe where my grandparents came from was potatoes, as in Ireland. Potato pancakes were eaten with pickled cucumber, with apple sauce, and even with mashed potato. After that you could eat them with sugar or apricot jam as a sweet. In German they were called Kartoffeln Pfuffer. In Yiddish they had the less unwieldy name of latkes. The ingredients are cheap; they are easy to make and yet a delicacy.

Here is a de-luxe version from Poland.

Krystyna's latkes (Potato pancakes)

Serves 8, or more as an accompaniment
6 medium potatoes
1 small sweet potato
1 medium onion
2 eggs
2 Tablespoons self-raising flour
salt, pepper
pinch dried marjoram
sunflower oil

Peel the potatoes and grate them together (ordinary and sweet). Drain off the surplus liquid (the drier they are, the lighter your latkes). Add a grated onion. (A food processor makes short work of all the grating and you don't risk grating your knuckles.) Mix in a beaten egg, flour, marjoram, salt and pepper (freshly ground). Fry tablespoons of the mixture in hot sunflower oil (1 tablespoon = 1 latke).

Flatten your latkes with a wooden spoon as they are frying, so that they are not too thick. Fry on both sides till crisp. You can eat them on their own.

I like them hot with cold sour cream or yoghourt mixed with chives.

Krystyna says you can eat them with Mexican Taco sauce. As my poor grandparents fled to England from the east, not the west, this was a refinement unknown to them.

A taste of poverty

Having been brought up in the East End of London during the slump, poverty has held few attractions for me. It is fruitful spiritually if you welcome it, it is not so productive if you just suffer it. Then it is just grind, and hanging on, for below you is the abyss of the homeless and the dispossessed.

The hostels of the Salvation Army are wonderful institutions, but I still tremble as I pass them, because at one stage of my life, I got a little too close. I was born in one.

Quite often in my life I lose things, because I am a vague person, who gets detached from things in a material rather than a spiritual way.

Bits seem to drop off me rather like bits of toe that dropped off King Louis Philippe, which his valet found in his sock. I part company with cheque-books, credit cards, pious pictures and recipe notes. I have kept my feet and my head, woolly though it is.

So life is one long drama of 'Hunt the Diary', and learning to reassemble the bits of me again. It is fortunate I decided to become a rabbi, and not a Queen's Messenger, for although we are told it is easy to lose one's soul, it is not so easy to mislay it.

Once I did lose everything. I had just been released from a theological meeting in Germany, and was invited as soon as I arrived in Holland to an exuberant party. I shed my coat, tie and gravitas and exchanged wisecracks with a lady stevedore while eating pickled cucumbers, washed down with gin. When I was about to go, I suddenly realized I had forgotten where I was going to. This didn't much matter as I had nothing to go with. My luggage had gone too and, as I found out later, was heading with some other guests to a camping site in one of the remoter regions of that country.

Who took the luggage I never knew. Since I do not even know their names, I am not able to ask them if my notes on Luther added to the happiness of their holiday, or whether my minister's dog-collars (one clean, one dirty, both plastic) looked *comme-il-faut* on the beach.

I ended up in the flat of a kindly publisher who though not of my faith, or any faith, took pity on me. He not only gave me a sleeping-bag and a towel, he also lent me his toothbrush, which I think is the highest rung of generosity (only two other people have ever lent theirs to me and both were in holy orders). It is easy to be magnanimous with cigarettes or bath salts, but how few will refurbish your underwear or your dentures.

Before I slept in my strange surroundings I wondered what I would eat if ever I indeed lost everything and returned to the poverty of my birth.

In the East of London in the depression potatoes formed the menu of poverty. We used to sing a song in Yiddish which went:

> Monday potatoes
> Tuesday potatoes
> Wednesday potatoes etc. etc. etc.
> And on Sabbath as a treat
> Guess what!
> A potato pudding.

Actually Eastern European Potato Pudding is a treat.

Potato Kugel

Grate the potatoes on a coarse grater. Drain off excess liquid. Add the salt, pepper, and milk beaten together with the eggs. Chop finely and fry a large onion till soft in the oil and add the onion and the oil to the potato mixture.

Pour it into an oiled baking-tin and bake it for about 1½ hrs at 325°F Gas 3 160°C. It should have a nice brown crust on top. Eat it with pickled cucumbers. You don't need meat – it is good enough on its own.

My grandmother used to separate the yolks and whites, and whisk the latter separately and fold them in. I don't have the time. The dish is called a Babka in Polish and a Kugel in Yiddish.

Serves 6
2lb potatoes, peeled
1 large onion
2 eggs
1 teacup milk
2 teaspoons salt
¼ teaspoon pepper
3 Tablespoons oil

Prancing clergy

One of the most dramatic moments of the Jewish liturgy takes place on the Day of Atonement, the holiest day in the year. The prayers rise to a crescendo of fervour as the Temple is remembered and the kingship of God proclaimed.

At that point the rabbi, flanked by two synagogue elders, falls on his knees and then prostrates himself before the Ark in submission to God.

After the prayer is over, the two helpers gently help him to his feet. It is the only time that prostration takes place in a synagogue.

Well, two years ago they tried to help me gently to my feet, but it was no go. The elders yanked but my prostration was not just liturgical, it was also medical. Something had gone in my back, and there I was prostrated now and for ever. They raised me somehow (rather like the *Mary Rose*) and I carried on with the service majestically upright in my pulpit. It looked rather solemn, because I couldn't move a muscle, but people like their religion rigid rather than *mouvementé*, which is disturbing.

Since every change of posture, every twitch was agony, I appeared for once in my life quite dignified. I could only roll my eyeballs, and pucker the corner of my lips into a sneer.

Well, the Day of Atonement is once again on the way, and when I'm flat, they will think the same words Galileo said aloud: '*Eppur si muove*' – 'and yet he moves' – but more as a question than a statement.

I am more hopeful this year as I have been learning the Alexander Method which teaches me how to walk and sit and carry things, and free my neck, and think upwards (physically, not morally).

Through freeing my neck and thinking upwards, I am inclined to prance rather than walk, like a show-jumping horse. Anyway, it's a noble gait even if it is a bit too proud for someone as uncertain as myself.

I have, however, found that changing my posture makes me more cheerful. So I smile as I prance.

I wonder if we think about our posture when we pray. I hate standing up and sitting down and can never understand why some people think you have to stand up when you sing. After all, I am not the Bach Choir – nor are you.

But enough. This article is about prancing not grousing. I certainly prance home in double time when this dish is waiting for me in the kitchen. I have grown very attached to it, and I learnt it from the Editor of *The Universe* herself.

Stuffed aubergines

Cover the aubergines with water, and simmer them for 20 minutes until soft. Meanwhile chop the onion and garlic and fry slowly in oil. Skin the tomatoes. (I have to admit I don't bother unless my guests are the finickity sort.) Slice the tomatoes and add to the onions. Cook until just soft. Slice the cheddar and stir into the mixture.

Remove the aubergines from the water and cool. Slice lengthways. Scoop out flesh, chop and stir into the onion–tomato mixture. Cook slowly for 10 minutes. Stir in the rosemary. Check seasoning.

Oil a baking tray and place the half-aubergines on it. Fill them with the mixture from the frying-pan. Sprinkle with Parmesan, and chopped olives if you have any.

Bake for 30 minutes at 350°F Gas 4 180°C.

Serves 4
2 medium aubergines (long not round shape; each one should make 2 'boats')
2 Tablespoons oil
1 small onion
2 cloves garlic
4 tomatoes
2oz Cheddar cheese (or cottage cheese if fresh)
½ teaspoon rosemary
grated Parmesan
olives (optional)

We are commanded to love our neighbours and what a jumbled and unlikely lot they are.

The word 'neighbour' doesn't mean someone who is like us, but someone whom God has placed next to us and God certainly has catholic tastes and a sense of humour.

Walking in my area of London, you will find Cypriot grocery shops next to Pakistani restaurants, and Indian vegetarian take-aways just by Chinese restaurants with delicious dead ducks turning and roasting away in the windows.

They are various and God commands us not just to like them or put up with them, but to love them and vice-versa, of course.

How do you learn to love? You can't take an evening course in loving, or get a B.Sc. in tolerance. It is something which has to grow in you like a seed and tact is a good way to begin.

All of them have different food rules and preferences and these are not arbitrary or faddy. Their menus are an expression of their theology and have to be treated with respect.

Moslems and Sikhs don't touch alcohol, because it affects their freedom and judgment, and freedom is God's most precious gift. It isn't as easy doing God's will if you are sozzled.

Jews don't eat pork or shellfish, because it says so in their scriptures either directly or implicitly. The home of the Holy Family was certainly a kosher one.

Very pious Indians will be strictly vegetarian, because they do not wish to kill a fellow creature. Some will even avoid milk products because the milk was intended for the calf, not for them. In any case if you believe in reincarnation or transmigration of souls the question of who was who or what, is sobering.

Some Catholic religious also never eat meat, and some are allowed to eat it when they go visiting.

All this does require mobility and imagination on the part of the cook. I had to do some fast thinking when two religious and vegetarian friends dropped in unexpectedly, just as I was about to produce roast beef and Yorkshire pudding.

I didn't have a nut cutlet handy, or a soya steak, only some bits of aged mousetrap cheese and stumps of dry Gruyère and Dutch Gouda. So I quickly put together the following recipe.

I quickly put a small pan in the hot oven with the vegetable oil.

While this was heating up, I made some more Yorkshire pudding batter with the flour, eggs, milk and water. I added the Marmite, mixed herbs and a good pinch of pepper. Then I had some sage and onion packet stuffing, which I made up into small balls.

I only had time to let the batter rest in the fridge about 10 minutes, but I have never been worried by a few little lumps. In the finished product you don't notice them.

I took out the pan with sizzling fat, threw in the cheese lumps trimmed into neat cubes, and stuffing balls and poured the herbed batter all over.

I put the pan back at the top of the oven and let it cook for 40 minutes at 375°F Gas 5 190°C. The result looked brown and tempting and smelt very nice as well.

Serves 4
4oz plain flour
2 small eggs
½ pint mixed milk and water
½ Tablespoon Marmite
½ teaspoon mixed herbs
**packet sage and onion
    stuffing**
4oz cheese (approx.)
2 Tablespoons vegetable oil
pepper

The roast-beef brigade got interested and insisted on a bite of it. They didn't believe in prejudice, they said, only in sharing, as they stole another forkful.

Prayer isn't . . .

We were on a retreat and each of us was asked to get a piece of paper and write on it the words, 'Prayer is . . .'. Then we were told to complete the sentence, fold the paper and drop it in a biscuit-box.

I stared at the words 'Prayer is . . .', sucked my pencil, watched other people write out their answers industriously, and decided it was all beyond me. I went on a walk and exchanged back-chat with some haughty sheep (not nearly as sympathetic as cows, and much more neurotic). I came back, took up the paper again and firmly wrote the words 'Prayer isn't . . .' and now there was no stopping. Prayer isn't being sweet, sixteen and soppy. I don't like prayers which just thank God for buttercups, daisies, brooks that babble, and preachers who do the same, without mentioning the less welcome bits of life as well.

Prayer isn't misusing Teresa of Avila as a Baedeker, and grimly trooping from room to room in the Interior Castle, remorselessly, systematically and clumsily. I am somewhere in the moat.

Prayer isn't blessing everyone and everything in sight or mind, because you're frightened you might leave someone out. That isn't charity; it's weak-mindedness. Inflated prayers are like inflated money. A lot of it gets you very little.

Prayer isn't mooning mindlessly in a muddle of memories. The past is not always poignant or precious, and an awful lot of letters need a dustbin, not pink ribbon.

All this is rather caustic, and the only explanation for it I can give you is that I am on a diet. But even if you can't consume food you can think about it and talk about it. A good eater should be able to read a recipe, like a musician reads a score.

I helped out on a prayer retreat with this cauliflower dish, for Poland and piety go well together.

It makes British (and Irish) cauliflower look anaemic, and only fit for burial under a mousetrap sauce.

Polish cauliflower

Boil the cauliflower florets so that they are done but still firm. Drain and put them in a hot dish. In a frying-pan soften in 2 tablespoons of butter, a medium finely-chopped onion. Add some more butter, and when it sizzles add a teacup of fresh white breadcrumbs. When they are light-brown, stir in 3 or 4 tablespoons of chopped parsley. Salt and pepper to taste, and pour the contents of the frying-pan over the cauliflower. Now finely chop a hard-boiled egg, and sprinkle this over the breadcrumbs.

Serves 5–6
1 large cauliflower
1 medium onion
3 Tablespoons butter
1 teacup fresh white breadcrumbs
3–4 Tablespoons chopped parsley
1 egg, hard-boiled
salt, pepper

It is a dish fit for a Queen or Pope, and if they should happen to read this column, and say 'Why! that would be perfect for tea at Windsor – a real Anglo-Polish-Jewish cauliflower tea,' then I should feel very proud.

Lament for lost ideals

For some years I tried to be a vegetarian, and finally gave up because I was too weak and the social pressures too strong. I might try again sometime, as after six-month plant purification, my only cravings were for liver, lights, bangers and burgers. This shocked me, because I thought I had better taste. But there it is. I didn't sigh for Stroganoff, or whisper for Filet Wellington, I just lusted for bangers, mash, and gravy with lots of onions (and even more).

Vegetarian restaurants were a various lot. Most were a delight – imaginative, helpful and efficient. I have very good memories of Guava Fool, and cheese 'steaks' coated in Dijon mustard and batter, and then fried in deep fat. The waitresses coddled me, because I was a potential convert to the cause, and because I seemed to eat more than anyone else. (Vegetarians seemed to be a lean lot, and I had been stuffed since childhood with chicken fat, goose fat, and salt beef.)

As a student I was truly grateful because they were cheap, and because I met the most amazing characters there. At lunchtime the learned flocked like lemmings from the British Museum library to lentils and nutmeat at a wonderful restaurant nearby. I chewed and I listened, and got food for my mind as well as my body at no extra cost. It was a good life.

There were of course other vegi restaurants, fortunately rare, which were like collapsed communes, after a revolution that went wrong.

You ate gritty delights on the barest of boards. The benches had no backs, and the moody waitresses (if there were any) slurped their gruesome gruel.

I rarely got a cloth napkin, and none I went to ever dealt in alcohol (vegetarian only!) to my satisfaction.

Here is a dish which I learnt from Gian-Carlo, an Italian friend. It can keep four students alive without too much trouble or expense if they are sage enough to grow a sage bush.

Gian-Carlo's sage spaghetti

Serves 4
¾–1lb spaghetti, tagliatelle
or fettucini
2–3oz butter
1 Tablespoon oil
3 sage leaves per person
salt, pepper
Parmesan or Cheddar cheese

You can experiment with other pastas such as tagliatelle or fettucine! When cooked but not soft – *al dente* – drain it well in a colander and keep it warm. Meanwhile melt 2 to 3oz of butter in a pan with 1 Tablespoon of oil so that it does not brown or blacken. Fry in it a handful of sage leaves till they are crisp. (I use about 3 per person.) Add salt and pepper, and pour over the pasta. Grind Parmesan cheese over it, but from a block not from a pot. If you can't get it from a block, use Cheddar. (I hasten to add this is my suggestion not Gian-Carlo's.)

I was trying so hard to be a vegetarian. After a meeting my fellow delegates went off to a juicy and bloody steak dinner. Feeling virtuous but empty, I too sought a juicy cutlet (nut) in that carnal and carnivorous city, where our conference was held.

It was not easy to find. Everybody knew a restaurant where they served vegetables. But only vegetables? They shook their heads. No gravy, no chops? I must be mad!

Finally I wound up in the cellar of a commune. I think they were a religious lot, but I never discovered what deity they worshipped (if any).

I relaxed as I went in. The diners didn't stare at me, or crudely point with their fingers. They just gazed sweetly ahead in their places, their chestnut ringlets (unisex) falling gently down, entwined with very semi-precious stones.

PLAT DU JOUR

COMPOST-
GROWN
POTATOES.. 60 p.
with
extra
COMPOST 75 p.

Menu

What was on the menu? I asked, and my neighbours' smiles just got sweeter. I felt uneasy. It seemed that everyone had seen a vision except me. In face of such goodness I felt very humble, and remained hungry and humble until one of the diners keeled over and passed out – stoned!

It was a curious culinary experience. The soup was lumpy with vegetables grown in compost, some of which was in the soup. The flavour was earthy as one would expect but rather good. In fact it would have been very good if it had not been burnt. I complained to the gentle waiter who apologized quietly, and then took the wind out of my sails by saying of course they never charged for soup.

I went to visit another commune where they taught me how to cook rice. We contemplated the rice for two and a half hours, and in the next half-hour we burnt it.

But I did learn some things. I became an addict of soya bean curd. You can get it in Far Eastern groceries and health food shops, and I think it can now be found in adventurous delicatessens and super-markets.

Fried Tofu

It is like a white custard with a lovely smooth texture, which doesn't taste of anything much, but what taste there is is rather delicate. Experiment with a tin or packet and ask for Tofu. If you refrigerate it for a day, the water will drain away, and the custard will firm up.

I cut it carefully (it is fragile) into slices, and dust them with seasoned flour and herbs. I use more salt than usual. I then fry the slices carefully in hot margarine and oil until they are brown. With fried eggs, tomatoes, mushrooms and Worcester sauce, they are delicious. Who would ever want b-c-n?

Down market

I could spend my life happily in a junk market, sorting through the débris of other people's lives.

I certainly spent one holiday doing just that. I had just finished my first job as a minister, and I was exhausted. So I sat by a stall in the Amsterdam 'flea market' on a packing-case and drowsed.

From time to time I tottered to the stall and bought a mug of coffee and a slice of Dutch apple cake.

Sometimes in a burst of energy I tottered to a further stall, and munched a matjes herring, holding it by the tail.

Stall-holders, bargain-hunters and beggars sat on the packing-cases near me, and the herring tail introduced me to a three-legged cat who became my mate for a fortnight. I couldn't take her back to England because of the quarantine laws (so I told myself) and because of my own cowardice.

As I got stronger and stopped thinking about people and problems, I began to wander among the stalls, picking up little treasures.

I found an old Victorian copy of Thomas à Kempis, and I still have it, having grown fond of the saccharine angels and the brightly coloured saints who decorate it. (They look like the sweets I was given as a child.)

I also found a photograph album of a family who looked Jewish. The pictures stop abruptly in the middle, and I cannot help thinking of the deportation centre close by the market. I no longer have it. Perhaps I did not want to keep it.

On a more practical level I acquired a box of cut-glass *messen-liggers* – little supports on which you rest your used cutlery without dirtying the tablecloth. On the continent you use less gear on better food.

I also found an old handwritten recipe book from the early years of Queen Wilhelmina. It opened itself at a page for cucumbers. My Dutch wasn't good enough to follow it exactly, but here is my version of *Haagsche Komkommers*, a dish which is easier to eat than pronounce.

Dutch cooked cucumber

Peel and seed the cucumber, and cut it into bite-sized pieces. Simmer them until they are almost soft, and drain them immediately. Now make up a white sauce by melting the margarine, and stirring in 2 tablespoons of plain flour.

Let it cook for 2 minutes. Then slowly add the milk and stock mixed. When the sauce is smooth and thick, season with salt and pepper, add the cucumber pieces, cream, chopped chives, tarragon and sugar. Heat the sauced cucumbers gently, sprinkle the top with a little freshly grated nutmeg and serve straight away.

Serves 4 as accompaniment; 2 as main dish
1 large cucumber
2 Tablespoons margarine
2 Tablespoons plain flour
¼ pint milk
¼ pint light stock
1 Tablespoon cream
1 Tablespoon chopped chives
pinch tarragon, sugar
pepper, salt
grated nutmeg

By the way the market is still there, but it has been moved to the other side of the Waterlooplein Square. The Catholic church of Moses and Aaron still overlooks it, as do the synagogues.

They don't have many packed services, however, for too many people lost their lives, and their faith, in the occupation.

COMPOSING SALADS

I had some paintings in an exhibition just as I was on my way out of university. My cheek was colossal, verging on the manic, because I seriously considered dedicating my life to Art on the strength of a tepid revue in a student magazine. I then decided I was too precious for the things of this world, and wanted to make my life a work of art and head for eternity instead. I am not at all surprised I ended up shortly afterwards on an analyst's couch. Looking back on it, the only thing that surprises me is that it took me so long to lie down.

But bits of the old urge surface now in a comfy domestic way, and I compose salads for friends. I feel creative as I put green bits on red bits, and scatter parsley everywhere. Their 'oohs' and 'aahs' as they see the dish on the table mean almost as much as a review, even though I realize that I am not a missed-over Miró or a passed-up Picasso.

Parties and guests

I have never minded providing the food for parties. In fact I enjoy it. But I do mind having to provide the entertainment at the same time. It is just not possible to bring in fresh supplies of food, check the drinks, and make sure that no one is fainting with embarrassment in a dark corner, or fading into the wallpaper from loneliness. It's the last straw, and ensures that the host cannot enjoy his or her own party, which is a shame, and even worse – bad manners.

At an 'open house party' some friends brought friends of friends, who were certainly no friends of mine. They were young, and uncertain of themselves, and that is hard. But instead of accepting their uncertainty, one or two of them (not all) tried to bluff it out, which rarely pays. Jokes are difficult if you are insecure, so they tried to be puritan and serious which is easier. As their motives were wrong, they only succeeded in seeming sulky and peevish.

It certainly ruined my party, and when they left, they wrote high-minded slogans on my wall. Righteousness is one thing, self-righteousness is another. May God keep me from ever confusing them.

It was nice to meet another generation at an elderly friend's. They passed things, and poured things, and chatted each other up.

They did justice to the cakes (and the washing-up). They didn't just talk about justice, they made sure their hosts had a slice too. Nothing profound was said, and the social comment whether left, right or centre was unoriginal.

But a party is a sort of game, and it is only politeness and decency to observe the rules. If you are invited for bridge, you don't insist on canasta!

One of the things which stood out when I first read the Gospels was the number of times Jesus was invited out. It's an odd thought, but He must have been rather good at parties.

Jesus and the Apostles were great fishers. Indeed the gospels end with a description of a fried fish barbecue breakfast by the shores of the Sea of Galilee – you can find it in the last chapter of St John's Gospel.

Here is a simple Summer Fish Salad, which is very nice for a hot climate. Jesus couldn't have eaten it though, because mayonnaise was not invented until modern times.

Summer fish salad

Poach the white fish fillets – you can use the burner or the oven – for about 15 minutes.

Let the fish cool, and flake it. Put the flakes into a serving dish.

Now sprinkle over them the chopped chives or spring onions, and fresh chopped herbs. Season.

Stir together the mayonnaise and the low-fat yoghourt, season and fold it into the fish and herbs. Sprinkle with fresh chopped parsley.

Serves 4–6
1½lb cod, haddock or halibut
½ cupful chopped chives or spring onions
¼ cup chopped fresh herbs
6–8oz jar mayonnaise
4oz carton low-fat yoghourt
chopped parsley
pepper, salt

Spiritual holidays

There are all sorts of books that tell you how to prepare for your holiday practically, but there are few books, or sermons for that matter, that tell you how to prepare for your holiday spiritually. Now I am no expert on the answers but I can at least set out the problems. Because I don't find taking a holiday very easy.

I asked a colleague of mine about holidays and he said, 'I don't go on them. I am not stable enough to cope with them.'

In normal life we are shielded by all the little fences and barriers we set up to protect ourselves from ourselves and others. On holiday there is an uninterrupted stretch of time in which we are asked to enjoy ourselves and be happy. The only interruptions are food and drink – which is why they are the main subjects of conversation.

Being happy is an art, and a spiritual art. It doesn't seem to come if you chase it. It steals up on you when you are thinking of something other than your own happiness. You run after happiness, and happiness runs after you.

Therefore the simple recipe for it brings disaster, and lots of people come home feeling cheated. Yes, they had three meals a day, and a balcony, and a sea view – but when they added them all up, the total was comfort. It wasn't happiness.

It is important to remember that happiness and contentment are internal states. They are not things. You can't get them out of a bottle – like a suntan, or streaks in your hair. Their ingredients are goodwill and a good conscience and no factory produces these, only God within you.

We also spend more time than usual with relatives and those we love. Our relationships with people close to us are more complex than most of us admit. I know lots of people who behave beautifully to everybody except their parents. I also know from experience that the first people I get irritated with are my nearest and dearest. After wonderful retreats when I thought I had reached a spiritual high, they have been my Waterloo. So recognize the dangers and be prepared.

How should you be prepared? The easiest way to anaesthetize problems is to drink them away in the local vino. It is an *ersatz* way of keeping everybody 'happy' which I do not advise. It is best to find a church or place of worship nearby and go every morning before breakfast. I should also like to recommend a few minutes at night as well, but alas the churches are locked.

I don't think you have to measure prayer by length, it isn't curtain tape or dress material. I find a few minutes of recollection quite enough. The important thing is: don't let up!

When I went on holiday to Italy I learnt that good food like good prayer can be very simple. My favourite dish required no cooking at all.

Mushrooms from Genoa

Wipe the mushrooms, slice them thinly, and carefully chop the parsley, garlic and herbs finely. Mix with the mushrooms, add a few grinds of fresh pepper, and pile on a platter. Salt very lightly.

Cut the anchovy fillets lengthwise into narrow strips and lattice them over the mushrooms. Dribble the oil all over.

Serves 4

1lb good quality button mushrooms – tight ones
handful of fresh parsley
1 fat clove garlic
3 Tablespoons fresh chopped herbs – if they are not fresh don't bother
salt and pepper
1 tin anchovy fillets in olive oil

Surprise, surprise!

An American friend of mine, who was studying in England recently, gave a dinner party. He spent two days on the cooking but unfortunately never considered the difference of taste which separates our countries as effectively as the Atlantic.

I entered with a conservative Englishman of the old school – I mean public school, which is private school in America. Our host was hurt to the quick by the Englishman's comment.

Gazing with awe at the mixture of pineapple and peanut butter (which was odd but delicious) and the devil's food cake, and fudge cake alongside it, he exclaimed: 'My God, it's the Teddy Bears' picnic!'

Now this is not a comment which makes for the success of such an evening. And all the Englishman's charm and contrition couldn't wipe it out.

I must admit that I do like sweets at the end of the meal, and I do not like them to surprise me by turning up as the first course. Do you really like the tinned mandarin orange and grapefruit segments turning up before the roast beef, or toad-in-the-hole?

In America I was first anaesthetized with strong martinis, and when I staggered to the table, we were all served strawberries in Tequila with whipped cream.

Occasionally you ask me if these grisly repasts are true. Well, yes, this one was. And very good it was too if only it had not been the overture to fishballs.

In Indian cooking the surprise comes at the end. If you go to an Indian restaurant, I suggest you ask to finish the meal with 'pan'. The owner will probably be charmed by your real feeling for Indian cuisine. You will receive a green leaf stuffed with spices. On the sub-continent the effect is strange and sometimes explosive. Over here it is curious and not disagreeable.

At some Jewish banquets I have attended, there was a nasty surprise of sneaking in milkless ice-cream somewhere between the fish and the meat. Whether this meant to convey a hint as to the frozen origin of the other courses I do not know.

Sometimes the 'ice-cream' was surprisingly good, but sometimes the result was as appetizing as a portion of sugared grey concrete turning up unexpectedly before the loyal toast. Where the notion for this came from I do not know.

For those who like the combination of sweet and savoury tastes combined, these simple salads will do nicely, though they do not have the transatlantic bravura.

Salads with sweetness

Peel and grate 1lb carrots and marinate them in orange juice. Stir in a handful of plumped raisins. Salt and pepper to taste, and scatter the carrots generously with cinnamon.

Another dish I like is melon and pimento. Cut the melon into chunks or balls and pour French dressing over it. Lattice the top with thin strips of tinned red pimento (if not tinned, parboil them first), and anchovy fillets, divided in two lengthwise. Both dishes benefit by being chilled.

Another good one! On a bed of watercress, arrange thin slices of avocado, orange and grapefruit segments, and peach slices. Pour over French dressing.

If you are fed up with French dressing over everything – here is a simple salad or *hors-d'oeuvre* which tastes better without it. Grill red and green sweet peppers under a hot grill, until they are charred. The skin can then be removed while they are hot – use gloves! Now remove the stalk core and seeds, and cut into strips. Serve with chilled natural yoghourt. They taste good and do you good because they are full of Vitamin C.

Cooking up art

A Jewish businessman, I was told, visited a modern art exhibition. Bewildered and bemused he stopped in front of a tastefully arranged posy of drain pipes and nervously and humbly asked, 'Is that art?'

Yes, he was assured that was not only art, it was art of the first quality. He looked at it doubtfully, shook his head, and was about to leave the gallery. Suddenly he turned. How much were the drain pipes? he asked. Two thousand guineas he was told.

Slowly he took off his hat. 'That', he said reverently, 'is Art!'

Now a lot of modern art has an entertainment value which an acre of Old Master does not possess. I like auto-destructive art, when the exhibits crumble, powder or burst into flames before your eyes. I am not quite sure I would buy one, even at a knock-down price. How would I insure it?

I also like art which, after viewing, the viewers can eat. I have never bitten into a Botticelli or licked a Leonardo so I cannot comment on their good taste. But I am game, and perhaps canvas is low on calories and high on polyunsaturates. I like Rubens, but I wonder what it would be like if you salted and peppered one of his buxom ladies, and then *bit* her.

I also like modern art I can clamber over, and fall into. The exhibits wouldn't fit into my sitting-room, but with any luck my sitting-room could fit into them. It would be nice to dwell in Culture.

This salad with its pale greens looks just as nice as a lot of exhibits at the Tate. After all you don't make a salad, you compose it! I have called it Special Composed Salad because it is not cheap. It is very good, and goes well after a heavy main course. It also suits people who don't like lettuce.

Special composed salad

Chop the celery into really small pieces. Squeeze the salty water out of the artichoke hearts and cut each one into 4 pieces. Wash, core and chop the pears (but do not peel them). Peel the cucumber and cut into 4 lengthways, then cut across to get small pieces. Wash and de-seed the grapes (it is better to buy seedless grapes, if possible). Combine all the salad ingredients in a bowl.

For the dressing, mix the dry ingredients first, then the mustard, then the vinegar and then the oil. Pour over the salad and stir well. The inventor of this salad warned me that the garlic tends to be rather strong, and can kill the gentler flavours; but some people do feel that no salad dressing is complete without it – including me.

Serves 4
Salad:
1 stick of celery
1 tin artichoke hearts
1 *small* **bunch white grapes**
1 large or 2 small pears
½ cucumber
Dressing:
1 teaspoon sugar
a good pinch black pepper
½ teaspoon salt
½ teaspoon made mustard
1 Tablespoon wine vinegar
1½ Tablespoons olive oil
1 crushed clove of garlic
(optional)

A touch of the exotic

My friend Isabelle is a wife, a mother, and a businesswoman. She does the shopping, drives a car, and gives superb, kind dinner-parties. Being Parisian they have to be elegant, and so does she. Paris is a lovely city but you have to be firm and well-organized to survive.

I enjoy watching Isabelle, petite, frail and feminine, overcoming tough lorry-drivers in her little Fiat, or rapidly considering a stall with 30 cheeses, and accurately selecting the one in best condition with an elegant unhesitating gloved finger. She is sympathetic, efficient, tactful, and very French.

Isabelle takes cooking seriously. She has little time, but everything has to be right. Isabelle also takes men who cook seriously, which English people don't. She does not take 'a bit of this' and 'a bit of that', or say, 'Don't worry, it all works out'. She gives me quantities exactly, and laboriously thinks if she has missed out any stage.

Here is one of her recipes which cooks itself. It doesn't come from France, but from North Africa opposite, just across the Mediterranean from Marseilles.

Couscous salad

Rinse the couscous in a colander and then empty it into a big bowl. It is a kind of semolina and you can buy it quite cheaply in any Middle Eastern or Greek grocery shop, and in a lot of supermarkets. Into the bowl add the tomatoes, peeled and roughly chopped, the cucumber peeled and cut small, the juice of all 7 lemons, the oil, chopped parsley, chopped chives, chopped mint, chopped onion, and crushed garlic.

Start off with 2 teaspoons of salt, and add more later to taste and at least 8 grinds of fresh pepper.

Mix it all together with a fork

Serves 8
1lb (500g) packet of couscous
¾lb tomatoes
1 cucumber
7 lemons
2 Tablespoons olive oil
2 Tablespoons veg oil
4 Tablespoons chopped parsley
1 Tablespoon chopped chives
2 Tablespoons chopped mint
1 onion, chopped
3 cloves garlic, crushed
2 teaspoons salt (add more to taste)
freshly ground pepper

and leave it in the fridge overnight,
covered.

The couscous will swell and 'cook'
in the lemon juice. Decorate it with
mint leaves. You will have a
colourful, filling, and exotic salad.

P.S. Isabelle is the wife of a rabbi, and a bomb went off outside her
synagogue in Paris. She now has many more cares, like all hard-
working women who struggle to keep life going in a time of violence.

Simple and natural

When I first started praying systematically and seriously, I confused
quantity with quality. With grim determination I ran laps round the
Liturgy, and told God all the things I thought He ought to hear. The
sentiments were heavy, and so was the style. I addressed Him as
'Thou' and got tied up in a cat's cradle of 'ests' and 'eths'. 'Thou
thinkest' and 'He acknowledgeth'. With my mouth contorted into a
ritual lisp, I tried hard to be unnatural, and hoped that God would
appreciate my intention if not the result. I had after all put a lot of
effort into my prayers, but was this effort duly noted on high? I had
my doubts.

God was certainly God, but was I really me? True prayer needed
both of us. It took me a long time before I told God my real feelings,
and prayed to Him about my real hopes and real fears, undistorted by
pseudo piety or respectability.

I suppose I just didn't trust Him enough. This was rather odd, as He
created me, the real me, not the me that looked better in other
people's eyes or even my own eyes.

Now I realize that the best place to start in prayer is from where
you are and from what you are. In fact for me it is the only place.

Cooking is similar. Other people's recipes need other people's pots
and pans, and other people's measures and minds. It takes a long
time before you can trust enough, so that a cookery book ceases to be
a jailer and becomes a friend. A compassionate recipe allows a
margin of error, and some scope for self-expression.

107

If you haven't had time to do much shopping, you can still fiddle around and make something quite succulent out of what you actually have.

Polish herring salad

Serves 6
½ pint mayonnaise
½ pint sour cream
1 teaspoon dill
1 cup cooked garden peas (if frozen, thaw out)
½lb carrots
½lb potatoes
¼lb French beans
1 small pickled cucumber
2 pickled herrings
½ medium onion
1 cooked beetroot
1 green-skinned apple
1 red-skinned apple
1 teaspoon capers
salt, pepper, sugar (optional)
a few mushrooms
1 hard-boiled egg
a few cocktail onions

Mix the mayonnaise, seasoned with dill, with the sour cream or ordinary cream whipped up, but not salad cream.

Fold into it carefully with a wooden spoon the peas, carrots (cooked and chopped), the potatoes boiled and cut into chunks (not the floury kind – new potatoes are fine), chopped, cooked French beans, cooked beetroot pieces, the onion minced, pickled cucumber (chopped), and pickled herrings cut into small pieces. Cut the green- and the red-skinned apples into chunks with their skin and mix with the capers.

Amalgamate, and add more mayonnaise and cream if required. Season with salt, pepper and a little sugar if liked.

Decorate with thin slices of mushroom and boiled egg, and with cocktail onions.

You can be simple in cooking as well as in prayer. Books on cooking or spirituality can be very useful, but sometimes it's better to lay them aside and just do what comes (super) naturally.

DRINKING

When I was evacuated during the war, I used to march against the Demon Drink. I sang lustily that 'My drink is water bright', and 'Hurrah for the pump hurrah, her blessings are pure and free'. I've forgotten the other words, but at the end I used to shout out 'And she is the dame for me'.

When I came back to London, I sang these songs to my grandfather, who listened to them gravely, and then cuffed me because he took them as a personal affront.

I don't get drunk, because I have always associated drink with religious festivals and social gatherings, and also because I fall asleep before anything can happen. I have met people who do, and it is saddening to watch the change of character it produces.

I like to hot up my tea with rum, and my coffee with whisky, but if I had to choose between beverages, I would plump for that childhood delight – Liquid bedroom bananas.

109

Super natural party

Loving those who love you is natural, loving those who don't is super natural. It's just as super natural as the Christian stories of a guiding star, or angels crying peace to shepherds, or animals kneeling in a manger. So instead of throwing a natural Christmas party throw a super natural one instead. The only difference is that you invite some of your enemies as well as your friends.

If you try hard enough, you might manage something better than a hard-fixed grin, and even rise to a genuine smile of amusement. There is nothing so disconcerting as turning the other cheek, if you don't hesitate and do it so quickly that it seems quite super-duper natural. If you do, and you have to think out if you are up to it, you won't have much time for the cooking, the group dynamics are going to be too important.

The first thing is to mellow your 'guests' without pickling them, so why not butter them up with Buttered Rum? Use mugs not glasses, and then you don't have to worry about them cracking.

You can let your friends and enemies assemble the contents of their own mugs. Then they can't hold you responsible. Don't get into a panic if there is no instant thaw, and don't throw in a bottle of cheap gin. You might not open their hearts, just Pandora's Box, and you need your Christmas too, not a couple of Panadol and a feeling of hatred for everyone, irrespective of race, religion or creed.

The next thing is to sweeten them up. I suggest a great fruit bowl, but give Golden Delicious and dates embalmed in sugar the miss. Fill the bowl instead with all those strange and lovely fruits you can get if you hunt them out – green Kiwis from New Zealand, very ripe Kaki, Chinese gooseberries or peeled lychees. They are so interesting that your guests will have something to talk about other than your actual or fancied misdeeds.

I should also bemuse your guests with the salad below, which is in a different dimension from mixed, green or exhausted. Serve it with French bread. The difference in textures and tastes is curious, and the garlic will make brothers of you all. If you can't muster enough mystical love, then try garlic instead. It is the lowest common denominator of human experience, but it too unites the human race.

Buttered rum

Put a generous tot of dark rum in each mug. Add butter, brown sugar, lemon juice, orange or lemon peel, and cinnamon.

Fill halfway up with boiling water.

per person
1 generous tot dark rum (at least 4 Tablespoons)
1 knob of butter
2 teaspoons brown sugar
1 Tablespoon lemon juice
strip of orange or lemon peel
1 inch stick cinnamon

Tuna with beans

Mix all the ingredients in a bowl.

With the oil from the anchovy and tuna tins make a cupful of sweetish French dressing, using cider or wine vinegar (1 part vinegar to 2 parts oil), add some salad oil if necessary. Pour over the other ingredients. Stir all together gently. Leave in a fridge overnight – taste and adjust pepper and salt (remember the anchovies).

The combination of flavours is rich and exciting. Serve it with French bread.

Serves 8–10
1 tin anchovies, chopped and drained (reserve the olive oil)
2 × 7½oz tins tuna, flaked and drained (reserve the oil)
4 large tins butter beans drained
1 small tin green lima beans
1 cucumber peeled, seeded and diced
1 small can red pimentoes, cut in strips
Green parts of 1 bunch of spring onions, snipped with scissors
1 teaspoon mixed herbs
10 grinds fresh pepper
2 cloves fresh garlic, crushed
1 small tin tomato purée
dressing
cider or wine vinegar
salad oil
1 teaspoon sugar

It is surprising what harmony can descend on a group of people at Christmas, if they are given a little push with rum, and are graced with garlic. So much friendship is reborn, you might well think that angels are mixing unseen among your guests. That's nice, and I should provide some angel cake for them. (Buy a mix.) But when you start seeing the angels, take an Alka-Seltzer and stick to lemonade.

When you start talking to the angels and handing them things, then ask a human being (no, not an angel!) to get you to bed. It's tough, but you aren't so super natural as you thought. And that is precisely what your enemies have been saying for years.

A tea to make marriages by

On an impulse I took a bus I hadn't jumped on for years, and travelled on it to the other side of London. I suddenly wanted to see where I was born, and to revisit the houses of my childhood. When I got there, I had to sit down on a bench to absorb the changes. I had expected some of the houses not to be there (I had seen them in flames in the blitz) but I hadn't expected the disappearance of whole streets and whole districts. The little houses I had once known had been sucked into the great blocks of apartments and duplexes and play areas which towered above me.

One of them I remembered well. In it lived a dignified portly gentleman who carried, flourished rather, a great red umbrella. He was the respected and pious marriage broker, who visited Jewish families on Sabbath afternoons.

While we children played at a distance, he discussed gravely the prospects of this boy or that girl. Were they suited? Was he pious enough for her? It had been heard, someone said, that he had drunk a cup of tea in a cinema under the influence of less observant friends. This was no light matter, and referred for anxious consultation. The rabbi must speak to him, and verify it. But what about her? She had beauty of heart but not form. Once again heads wagged. Her family must improve upon nature so that the commandment could be fulfilled – 'to be fruitful and multiply and replenish the face of the earth'. They would give her a dowry, a little business which would increase her attractions, and restore the harmony of the universe.

So the murmur of marital chatter filled the hours that led to twilight, when three stars appeared in the sky, and the benedictions were made, and the Sabbath departed.

As the marriage broker was a very important person in this little world he was not given ordinary tea from the brown earthenware betsy pot, but a glass of something really special. And this is what it was. Grand tea for us did not mean milk or cream but a headier mixture of rum, cinnamon and lemon. This is the hot version for winter.

Matchmakers' tea

Make a pot of Indian tea. Into each cup, put 1 inch cinnamon stick, 1 slice lemon, 1 Tablespoon lemon juice, 2 teaspoons sugar, and 3 Tablespoons rum. Pour in the tea.

In summer fill the cups with ice cubes as well as the above and pour strong tea over (the ice will dilute the tea).

Either way it helps you love your neighbour as yourself. After 2 cups it's not so easy to tell the difference.

Serves 4
1 pot strong Indian tea
4 inch sticks cinnamon
4 slices lemon
4 Tablespoons lemon juice
8 teaspoons sugar or more to taste
12 Tablespoons rum

Colour in the morning

As you gather more experience of life, you learn to simplify, so that you control household chores, and they cease to tyrannize you. Quite late in life I decided to rationalize bed-making. I've never been good at it, and it's a hopeless job for one. As you get one side tucked in, the other side comes out, and you feel like a human yoyo or a pendulum darting from one side to the other trying to control four edges at once, which is a logical impossibility.

To avoid all this, I learned not to make beds but to disguise them. A few tweaks and some pulls could do wonders for the naked eye, but not for the naked anything else. After I jumped into bed in the dark, and was impaled on a hidden fork, I decided I could no longer take the rough with the smooth and something would have to be done. Regretfully I scrapped all the blankets of a bygone age ('blankets are so healthy') and invested in a duvet and a fitted sheet. The result is snug and blissful. One pull and the sheet is flat, and my duvet does not need to be made, only patted.

I decided to get covers which were neither tasteful nor elegant, and which didn't match or 'go with' anything, except my mood – no pink roses, pale stripes in the sunset, or spring nosegays all in ghastly good taste. Instead I got one set of pillar-box red with salmon, green and blue stripes, and a 'Starwars' set. I contemplate them in the morning, and they take away life's greyness. It isn't easy to be pessimistic when you are dazzled by six feet of pillar-box and salmon.

In the Psalms, there is quite a lot about praying and contemplating in the night seasons. And bed is a very good place for such things. I let my mind roam over the events of the day, and try to see them differently, not through my own eyes this time but God's. It's also a good time to make peace with yourself, and giggle about people and events which seemed so important when you were vertical, and so silly now you are horizontal. The prayers in New Testament times often spoke of death as a going to sleep, and waking in the morning as a foretaste of resurrection.

Now to what you can consume while you commune in a prone position. Certainly nothing which requires such lethal instruments as forks. I suggest a chilled banana cocktail: luxurious but cheap.

Bananas in bed

Blend in an electric blender, pour into a long glass, and sip.

Serves 2
1 pint chilled milk
2 ripe bananas
2 small eggs (raw)
2 Tablespoons castor sugar
 (or to taste)
½ teaspoon of vanilla
grating of nutmeg

It serves as supper, a nightcap or breakfast, which is a great advantage. If you think life's tough, and you need some spoiling then add a dollop of vanilla ice-cream, or bite into a choc-ice at the same time. Your bedding will almost certainly have to go to the launderette, but then you can wake in the morning to a Thing from Outer Space.

SWEETNESS IS ALL

I don't go for diet desserts. If you are going to sin you might as well sin big, 'Dallas' or 'Dynasty' style. You will endure the same nemesis and low-fat yoghourt for the rest of the week whether you mix saccharine in the sugar or not. As one of the rabbis said: 'God's business is forgiving sins, and He prefers forgiving big ones to little ones.' I have therefore included all my favourites, chestnuts, chocolate, whipped cream and bananas. The only reason I have not included puddings is because I haven't got time to steam them. Yet a boiled pudding, filled with lemon, brown sugar and butter, all cooked to a toffeeish syrup, is still my greatest kitchen treat.

Abelard said that Heaven was the place where we got everything we ever wanted, and when we got it, it would be as lovely as when we

I don't know why SOAP OPERAS remind me of food — perhaps it's all that EATING one's words..

DALLAS

still wanted it. Well I don't want to eat Leviathan or be waited on by sloe-eyed virgins, though such are among the rewards of paradise promised us by some clerics. I'll just have another portion of that pudding please, whatever the effect on my spiritual body.

Anyway you have been warned, and what you do with this section is your business.

Personal list of happiness

Recently a friend of mine who is a graphologist read to me something she had written which moved me deeply. When life gets her down, she said, she made a list of all the things that made her happy. As I listened to her list, I drew up a canticle of all the things I had ever loved.

To make a list like this, one that really moves other people, you have to be very honest with yourself. It's no use listing things that ought to make you happy but don't, but the things which actually make you happy. I tried it, and it's not so easy.

These are some of the things which make me happy.

– Taking a service in a synagogue when there is hardly anybody there and God seems to make the few of you a family.

– Getting the first Underground train of the day, and feeling the excitement of an awakening city, and the club feeling of all the people in the carriage.

– Giving a coin to a beggar who seems pleased.

– Ditto to a waiter.

– A chocolate bar sandwiched between slices of buttered white bread.

– Ella Fitzgerald singing *Manhattan*.

– Me singing *Rosenkavalier* (all parts) under the shower.

– Running with a dog – pretending to myself that I am a dog – stealing a Dog Choc.

– Finding a postcard which saves me having to write a letter.

– Munching a raw onion.

– Praying with Novices, and getting a lift.

– Cooked bananas.

Yes, you've seen it coming. Here is a recipe to use up all the Shrove Tuesday pancakes you didn't eat, and stacked away (sandwiched with greaseproof paper, I hope) in your fridge or freezer. I don't know

116

whether they are in the spirit of Lent (I think they are within the letter).

If you are suffering from scruples as well as greyness (the two can go together), then check with your parish priest. He might just look at you, and tell you to have another.

Lemon and banana pancakes

Use up any old pancakes like this. Spread them with lemon curd. Wrap them around bananas, and put them in a buttered oven dish alongside each other. Sprinkle with lemon zest, and lemon juice. Dot with butter and bake for half an hour at 325°F Gas 3 160°C. Sprinkle with castor or icing sugar before serving.

Short and rather sweet

Someone sent me a prayer for my kitchen. It is one of the nicest presents I've ever received, and whoever you are who sent it (I don't know your name) I should like to tell you that it is hung up by my larder, and I glance at it before breakfast, and whilst making supper every day.

I don't think I'm the sort of person to storm the ramparts of Heaven. My heroic virtues are minuscule to the point of invisibility and I wobble physically and spiritually. But I can (while wobbling) just turn my neck a little, and for a moment try to gaze at God, and not at myself.

It's easier to move one's eyes that little fraction, if there is a nice framed prayer to look at. Anyway that's my recipe of salvation for wobblers. If you can't pray very much, and your meditation is more like rockcake than an éclair, just look at God for a moment whenever you can. He then might look back at you and into you. But that, dear reader, is quite another thing and beyond the scope of cookery.

I don't think the profoundest things in life are matters of length. A prayer is not holy chewing-gum and you don't have to see how far you can stretch it. Nor do you have to recite the whole book of psalms. An odd word or a short text often gets to the heart of the matter.

Sometimes a deep friendship is created in a very few minutes and you may never meet again. I met an elderly lady in a bus-station waiting-room. We spoke together about God, old age, love, sex and ambition. It lasted about 17 minutes – I know because the bus arrived on time – but we truly met.

The meeting had no before and no after but it was deep. So I like short texts like 'You are the salt of the earth' from St Matthew or 'the beggar's dog, and widow's cat, feed them and you will grow fat', by William Blake.

And now for a short rich recipe, which is an answer to your prayer, if you are giving a dinner party on the trot. It deserves a short, sincere and uncomplicated grace.

Chestnut pyramid

Serves 8
1lb tin of sweet chestnut purée
¼–½lb unsalted cream cheese or curd cheese
4 Tablespoons whipped cream
½ teaspoon vanilla
4oz dark melted chocolate or cocoa powder

Sweetened chestnut purée is cheaper than you might think. Mix it with the unsalted cream cheese according to taste, whipped cream, and vanilla. Form it into one pyramid, and then pour over it melted dark chocolate, or cover it with sweet cocoa-powder.

It is good enough for a dinner party, and provided you haven't lost the tin-opener it takes only five minutes.

It is very rich, and so the portions should be small.

If you are on a diet, you could substitute curd cheese – or forget it, because the calories are still colossal.

Serve with boudoir biscuits.

Celebrating with a family

I once spent Christmas with a family in Germany. I had got to know their relations who were studying in London, and with some hesitation they invited me. With some hesitation I accepted, for it was in the post-war years when there was a barrier of silence between Germans and Jews.

They had Christmas wreaths on the doors, and we waited in the sitting-room until the dining-room door opened. The room was dark except for the candles on the tree, and the music of Mozart drifted towards us, faint at first and then louder. Little gleaming angels peeped between the china. It was magic.

They had a passion for British foods, and I brought Earl Grey tea, and Worcester sauce and Stilton for the feast. They made me *Stollen* in return, which is a light German version of a Christmas Cake or Pudding.

I remember eating slices of *Stollen* with Glühwein, which sounds nasty like medicine, but is a lovely mulled wine. We were so relaxed, we even managed to discuss the last war – for me for the first time.

If I ever go there again, I would give them a taste of modern Jewish life in return. This avocado dessert is trouble free and unusual. As avocados are now cheap and plentiful, this sweet presents no problem.

Avocado dessert

Mash or blend the avocado, lemon, sugar and vanilla essence. Stir in the cream. Spoon the mixture into glasses, and decorate with flaked almonds or lemon and orange slices. Make it shortly before you eat it or the avocados might discolour.

Serves 4 large portions or 6 sensible ones

flesh of 2 ripe avocados
juice of ½ lemon and its grated zest
4 Tablespoons castor sugar
½ teaspoon vanilla essence
½ pint whipped double cream

The perils of house hunting

I have been house-hunting with friends and it is a dispiriting pastime. Either the rooms are right but the price is wrong, or both are right and the walls are collapsing with rot. It is just another illustration of the fact that what we want from life and what we get from it are very different, and you need a lot of religion to bear this with quietness of spirit.

As a child in the depression I used to stand in front of Nestlé's chocolate machines and wonder if adults would ever invent a machine where you could get the chocolate out without putting the penny in.

Well, it certainly doesn't exist in this life and I'm not sure if it exists in eternal life either – you would have to ask a theologian who is a specialist in chocolate machines. Anyway, surveyors' reports, like visits to the dentist, incline you to spirituality because they impress on your mind the temporary nature of the most solid buildings, the reality of pain and suffering, and the vanity of human desire, and that you will agree is quite a package.

My grandparents, like their pious friends, used to leave a little corner of their living-room unplastered to remind themselves that here is no abiding city and of that ominous text: 'unless the Lord build the house, they labour in vain who build it'.

When you are house-hunting this seems so patently true, it makes you weep.

It is a fact that all the ancient kings of Israel, who were great builders, were naughty or nasty, and only the ones who left no memorial behind or didn't have the energy to leave a memorial behind, figure in the piety stakes. Journeying through the Holy Land, you are always tripping up over bits of Herod, and their poor opinion of him is one thing that unites both Jews and Christians.

But let us return to pleasanter things like a pudding, which can comfort us greatly in this vale of tears. Here is a sort of Yorkshire pudding but in a sweet form which Yorkshire wouldn't recognize.

French batter fruit pudding

Serves 4–6

1lb fruit (cherries, plums or apples etc.)
4oz plain flour
3oz castor sugar
¾ pint milk
4 eggs
½ teaspoon vanilla flavouring

Take any stones and stalks from the fruit. Cut it up and place it in a generously buttered flattish baking dish. Make a batter of the other ingredients, stirring the eggs into the dry ingredients, and gradually add the milk to avoid lumps. Stir in vanilla. Pour the batter over the fruit, and bake in a moderate oven (350°F Gas 4 180°C) for about 45 minutes until set and the top is brown.

Eat it after another go at house hunting and comfort yourself with the fact that your eternal home has many mansions, and no dry rot.

Art melon

When you have installed the fridge take a plug out of the end of a melon. Remove the seeds. Fill with cut up strawberries. Pour over strawberry jelly made with half the amount of water given on the package. Pour into the melon. Replace the plug and chill overnight. Cut into quarters or into thick slices. If you are crazed by ambition, peel the melon, making sure you don't puncture the shell (the jelly will then drip out all over your fridge). Cover the melon with sweetened whipped cream, dotted with strawberries.

Today's special

As you get on in life, you begin to crumble – at least I do – rather like a stale sponge cake. And the bit of me that's crumbling at the moment is a disc in my vertebrae. So I am lying flat on my back, looking at some interesting cracks on the ceiling, and writing with a pencil, because ball-points don't seem to work upside-down. (Mind you, they never seem to work with me even the right way up.)

I've been puzzling over the etiquette of the sick bed. I want to ring up my friends and ask them what's going on. But if I do, and they ask what's happening to me and I tell them, there is often a pause and a suggestion of blackmail in the air.

A sick person is in a very strong position. The nice friends feel guilty. They feel they should postpone the shopping, the launderette and the baby, buy the regulation chocolate, and rush over.

I think a sick person doesn't want to disrupt other people's lives, but needs reassurance more than chocolate. You want to know that some friends are committed friends, and will always come if they are really needed. This is especially true if you are not married.

Another problem! What on earth do you do with a mounting pile of chocolate creams? Since every doctor counsels me to lose weight, the sight of them, sweet, soft and delicious, rouses me to fury. It's so nice if someone gives you a present of their labour, not of their money. A friend who makes you something elegant and fitting is a friend indeed.

This delicate sweet is no trouble to make but looks inviting. It is all whiteness.

Blanc

Make a little plateau of unsalted cream cheese and put it on a pretty plate. Dust it with a little sugar.

On top put some natural yoghourt and dust again with a little sugar.

Crown it with a blob of whipped cream.

Surround the layered whiteness with fresh strawberries or black and red currants.

You need something special in bed.

Matter of calculation

The Bible says that the 'Day of blowing the trumpet', i.e. the New Year, begins on the first day of the seventh month, which is very odd if you think about it (Numbers 29:1). Surely a new year should begin on the first day of the first month?

I don't think the ancient Hebrews were hot stuff at calendars, because the Scriptures describe different dates and calendars which do not tally. In the end they adopted the system of the Babylonians who were great star-gazers (they worshipped them) and were much better at it. It's only fair to add that the rabbis refined the Babylonian system and today it is a very accurate system indeed.

Unlike the Gregorian calendar, its months are based on the moon not the sun, so the dates in the two calendars never match and theologians have to be careful that Passover doesn't jump into Easter.

There is a tradition among Jews to eat something sweet on the New Year, so that the coming months will be full of sweetness. So after saying the festival blessing over the bread and wine, blessings are often said over apples and honey too. People also make honey cakes and there is much passing around and nibbling among friends.

I honestly have no time to make cakes on the New Year, as I am busy taking services. But my guests expect honey, so this simple sweet is festive and trouble-free. There is enough alcohol to stifle criticism, and as they eat it, it helps them to wish each other an equally sweet new year.

Babylonian honey sweet

Buy a honey cake (or a ginger or marmalade cake). Cut a thin slice from the top to remove any crust, and poke holes in it (borrow a knitting needle, but not a ballpoint). Now pour over it and into the holes the sweet dark rum. Cover it with sweetened whipped cream mixed with cream cheese. Dot it with walnuts, angelica, and cherries (when it begins to resemble a child's birthday treat, desist).

It looks and tastes quite something. If you can't wait for September (the Jewish religious New Year) or January (the secular one) then make it now and feel a bit Babylonian.

Serves 6
1 honey cake
½ mug sweet dark rum
1 teaspoon sugar
½ pint whipped cream
2oz cream cheese
walnut halves
angelica
glacé cherries

My father's bananas

I peeped inside a Job Centre some days ago. It was smart and elegant, not at all like the dreary Labour Exchanges of my childhood before the war. Some people were in it, carefully looking over the job details. They didn't have the depressed and defeated look I remember still after all these years. Probably they don't show their feelings now, but they must still have them. There is an awful lost feeling when you are in-between jobs and the elegant office doesn't take that away.

My father was unemployed for several years after the great Depression. It nearly broke him, for it took away his pride, and he was a proud man. Occasionally, he would get a few days' work selling ice-cream in the early spring or the late autumn. I used to trot along beside his ice-cream cart to keep his spirits up, for who wants a choc-ice in October?

My father was only a frying-pan cook, but one simple dish made us all hungry. He had learnt it from an old night-watchman who had a brazier.

We used to eat it around the kitchen table before I was sent to bed. My mother banged away on an old piano, my father did conjuring tricks, and we forgot the Depression and Oswald Mosley, and our poverty while we shared the last of my father's bananas.

Baked bananas

Put the slightly under-ripe bananas in a hot oven for 20 minutes (about 375°F Gas 5 190°C). Leave their skins on. The skins will turn black, but don't worry!

Take the bananas out of the oven. Everybody unzips their own. Sprinkle the bananas with castor sugar, butter, cream and lemon juice, and eat them piping hot. Icing sugar melts faster, but I prefer castor sugar. We never had butter because we couldn't afford it. This is one of nature's great treats, fit for a party as well as for a poor family in the Depression.

Serves 4
**4 under-ripe bananas,
   unskinned
castor sugar to taste
butter and/or cream to taste
2 lemons**

CELEBRATIONS

Like many religious professionals, I cope with festivals, but I can't really enjoy them. In any case the great religious truths don't have to be celebrated, they are the daily bread of ordinary life, if you want to live with integrity. I think it is non-believers, or unbelievers, or those who make a living out of them, who make them so important. There is now too much role-playing and too much 'Auld Lang Syne' for spiritual comfort.

As the religious crisis in Judaism has deepened, there has been an increase in folkways, and dinky pietism. Looking through the colour supplements of the newspapers there seems to be a Christian equivalent. Look at all those wreaths festooned around the carriage-lamps in the neo-Georgian doorways.

Still I like religious parties, and I don't mind catering for them if I like the guests, and if I don't like them, well it is a spiritual exercise. Now I know this is killjoy stuff, but it is a professional hazard. After you have demonstrated the Passover Home Service to earnest Christians, bored schoolchildren, Sunday School children, and flustered housewives using the same jokes on all, you get a bit queasy and antisocial, and the service becomes like those words I used to repeat over and over again as a child until they lost all meaning.

But like everybody else, I draw up lists, send cards, muddling addresses and work out who is worthy of an expensive card, and who loves me too much to think about grading. I wander round department stores and tie myself up with sticky tape, while the parcels come apart. And I cook and I pray, and sometimes both come out right in my kitchen, and then before the doorbell starts to ring some wonder stirs in my heart too, and I stir the sauce with rising hope and interest.

Celebrating on the cheap

It can be tremendous fun! But you do need a strong umbrella, a good pair of walking-shoes and imagination. Go to a street market at the last moment you dare, join in the quick sales and 'dutch' auctions. (You will discover the use of the umbrella), and be charitable about the bargains which got away.

If you are going to have Christmas or any festival on the cheap, you do have to come clean and be honest with yourself; do you really like heavy pudding? Do you find roast turkey corpse rather dull? Perhaps you could dispense with the bird and keep the stuffing – I would. This accompaniment, for example, is good enough on its own.

Orange rice

Mix together the rice, water, orange juice and salt. Bring to the boil, cover and simmer for 20 to 25 minutes until the rice is cooked. Add the remaining ingredients. Serve it hot. It doesn't need the bird.

Serves 10
1½ mugs raw rice (long grain)
½ mug water
2 mugs natural orange juice
1 teaspoon salt
1 teaspoon grated orange rind
½ teaspoon sugar
3 Tablespoons margarine
3 Tablespoons seedless raisins

Festive baked apples

Instead of Christmas pudding, have baked apples, cored and stuffed with chopped dates and mincemeat. The apples should stand in puddles of sweet cider in a buttered baking tin. (Don't forget to make a slit around the apples.)

You can put large dabs of *ersatz* 'rum butter' on top of the apples when they are served.

Rum butter

Beat the grated zest and juice of one orange into the margarine, creamed with the brown sugar. Beat in a few drops of rum essence to taste and chill.

Serves 4
4oz margarine
2oz brown sugar
1 orange
rum essence to taste

Now this is Christmas on the cheap, and you need effrontery as well as an umbrella.

But don't lose heart! The result can be more tempting than the old selection of greasy goodies lying in state round the dead bird, and unflavoured with imagination.

After all, I doubt whether the Holy Family shopped at the Nazareth Harrods or in the Bethlehem Bond Street. They probably just went to a street market just like you if they celebrated Christmas, that is. Now did they . . . I wonder . . . Ask Father!

Christmas is also for grown-ups

Your children are now grown-up and coping with their children. So you no longer have to wear paper-hats and false beards, or strain at crackers which only crack for Mr Atlas. You can talk normally. You don't have to use your special 'kiddie' voice – 'Let's all be bunnies!' You and your husband can now invite a civilized, contemporary, and fastidious couple like yourselves to dine at Christmas. You still love your children, of course, but you don't have to suffer their children's children gastronomically. Away with lollipops, jujubes and carbohydrates. On with the port and ripe Camembert, just beginning to ooze. It's so nice to be one's own age, and not have to act another.

Celery and potato purée will make a nice change from roast vegetables, and is much lighter.

Celery and potato purée

Clean, trim, and cut up a head of celery (no leaves or root or woody bits). Boil in salted water for 20 minutes. In fresh water boil the celery again with potatoes, peeled and quartered, till the potatoes are soft – another 20 minutes. Drain and mash with butter, double cream, salt and pepper.

This makes a nice accompaniment to the bird. But I do not suggest a monster turkey, as large and as appetizing as a lorry, but a crisp duck, which is just right for four. You can serve it with a cherry sauce.

Serves 4
1 head celery
1lb potatoes
2oz butter
**3–4 Tablespoons double
  cream**
salt, pepper

Cherry sauce

This is made from a large tin of stoned cherries, thickening the syrup with arrowroot and flavouring it with port.

Port jelly

Don't part from the port bottle, and don't drink it absentmindedly, because you are going to need it for the sweet, a lot of it in fact, almost a pint. Duck is rich, and your stomach is now a tender, delicate thing. So soothe it and pamper it with a 'port' jelly made (not flavoured) with real port not water.

And now for that nice Camembert on the ooze. 'What! You are feeling a little . . . Yes, I know what you mean . . . Of course I'll take it away . . . No, the cat won't eat it . . . Oh Lord . . . First on the right upstairs! . . . Margaret, open the door quick for Mr . . . Oh, no!'

Title of respect

A lady wrote me a complimentary letter. Yes, she enjoyed my cookery she said, and now made herself egg nog to face the despair that comes with dawn. But, she was curious, what did my title mean, what is a rabbi, and what is its origin?

I shall try to explain but a clear answer isn't easy. Nevertheless it's worth delving into, because Jesus was often addressed as Rabbi especially in St Mark's Gospel, and though he doesn't use it of himself, he doesn't reject it. The word literally means 'my master', 'my sir', or 'my teacher'. It is a title of respect rather like 'Monsignor' in the Catholic Church.

Rabbis are latecomers in the 4,000 years of Jewish history. They are not mentioned in the Hebrew Scriptures, and are only there for the second two millennia. Some of the greatest 'rabbis' never used the title at all.

Hillel, for example, lived before the time of Jesus. He was the author of the Golden Rule, and this tale is told of him. An idol worshipper asked him to sum up religion while he, the idolater, 'stood on one leg' – i.e., in an instant. Hillel answered, 'Don't do to your neighbour what you would dislike done to you. The rest is commentary, but you had better go and learn it.' Hillel never used a title.

I once asked my rabbi about this and he said, 'Even a title can sometimes be vulgar, but the absence of a title can never be vulgar.'

Rabbis are not priests, and have no sacramental functions, so their work is different from that of Christian clergy. They are not strictly necessary at any service, even if it is for confirmation, marriage or burial. As a learned layman is quite qualified to take over, what are rabbis good for, then?

Well, they are experts in religious law and three of them together form a court which can give a binding decision or ruling. As Jews are an argumentative lot, and there is no hierarchy, only time sorts out the disagreements. Where there are two rabbis, there are always three opinions – at least.

A rabbinical student, it is said, had a dream, and in his dream the Almighty appeared to him and told him he would become an influential rabbi. The student told this to his teacher. 'Pray', said his teacher, 'that the Almighty appears in the dreams of others and persuades them to become your followers'.

129

In the course of my ecumenical meetings, I have noted that all my colleagues, Christian and Jewish, are addicted to sweet things, like chocolates and sticky buns.

Here is a Jewish Passover sweet paste called Charoset, which represents the mortar which the Children of Israel used when they built the pyramids for Pharaoh in Egypt. It tastes very nice, even though it is a memory of slavery.

Every Jewish family has its own recipe. This comes from my colleague Rabbi Hugo Gryn. At Passover Hugo and Jackie Gryn keep open house, so their charoset is made in vast quantities.

Charoset

Serves 15

2lb assorted dessert apples (Coxes, Granny Smith, Russets, Golden Delicious)
1½lb assorted nuts (walnuts, hazelnuts, almonds but not peanuts)
1 teacup honey and sugar in any proportion
1 teacup sweet red Kosher wine, or more
1 Tablespoon cinnamon – or to taste
a dash of brandy

Chop or grate the nuts. Peel and grate the apples. (A food processor will release you from this modern servitude, if it is a servitude, that is. I often enjoy the work, and think about the festival as I do it.) Mix the apples and the nuts. Add the sugar honey mixture and the cinnamon. Add enough wine until the mortar texture is effected, i.e., spreadable paste. Pep it up with a dash of brandy.

It is odd to think that this was eaten at the Last Supper, but the tradition for it at Passover is old.

This amount will serve a large, extended and distended Jewish family – say 15.

How do you eat your Charoset? With buttered matza, digestive biscuits, on celery, and you can even mix it with your muesli – but not in front of the children – remember all that brandy.

Don't mix – and have a perfect party!

Invasion! 40 guests. 'Please drop in at Christmas!' You didn't mean it, so you felt guilty (quite rightly) and therefore added (quite foolishly) – 'Why not come for supper on Christmas day?' (Oy Vay!)

Well, Christmas Day has come, and so has your old pal 'Nemesis' with 40 not-quite-wanted guests. It's no good blaming your family, or chasing the cat – you did it, and you will have to make the best of it.

Here are some ground rules if you want to enjoy your own party, and why shouldn't you? Don't muck about with 'Punch' or 'Cup', and don't bother to adulterate the gin with fruit cocktail or golden syrup. Your guests will rightly despise you.

They won't know how strong your brew is, and nor will you, as you will always be adding more gin or pineapple bits. They will either remain sober and resent you, or they will be sick over your carpet and you will resent them. Worse still, you might be sick at your own party, and die of shame, and in bad odour. It happened to me.

You can't get out of the food, nor should you. But don't be a perfectionist, don't use your best china or glass, and don't make lots of little fiddly dishes, just troughs of big sustaining ones. Guests should be able to use spoons and bowls. You can't handle a knife and fork standing up.

You can prepare all these beforehand, and lots of guests at this type of gastronomic scrimmage enjoy milling around the kitchen timing things, and poking about in your drawers.

Bake pricked chestnuts on trays in the oven – 400°F Gas 6 200°C for about 20 minutes.

Buy a half Stilton, and let them dig in with spoons, classy and tasty. Use digestive biscuits (not chocolate) rather than cheese biscuits.

Put together great casseroles of Oeufs à la tripe the day before, and bake them as required.

Oeufs à la tripe

Hard-boil 2 eggs per person, and then halve them. (The only 'tripe' in this recipe is in the name.)

Peel and chop 1 large onion per person and stew them in a little lake of marge until soft. With flour and milk turn them into a thickish white onion sauce.

Enrich it with any combination of the following: evaporated milk, any cream you have over, tinned or fresh, packets of onion sauce mix, tins of condensed white onion soup or boiled onion purée or powdered milk. It should be thick but not solid.

Flavour it with nutmeg, mace, mustard, salt, and freshly ground pepper. When you have a trough of seasoned onion sauce, fold in the halved eggs.

Decorate the top with strips of cooked red and green pimento to give the dishes a cheerful Christmas look. You can prepare it all the day before, and leave it in the fridge. Heat the dishes as required in the oven for the party.

Serves 10
20 hard-boiled eggs
10 large onions
4oz margarine or butter
2 pints milk
4oz flour
nutmeg, mace, mustard
salt, pepper
red and green pimento
optional ingredients:
evaporated milk
cream
onion sauce mix
condensed onion soup
boiled onion purée
powdered milk

Dried fruit salad

For the sweet, I would shrug my shoulders and let it make itself. It can, you know! A day before, soak as many varieties of dried fruit as you can get in a scented china tea (sultanas, prunes, apricots, apples, pears, peaches, etc. – get the idea!). Add honey, almond flakes, orange blossom water and spoonfuls of yellow jam, e.g. yellow plum, apricot, or apple jelly. Let it soak for a whole day. Serve it in its juice with cream. As there is no cooking, the fruit is crisp and bitey.

And when they have all gone, and stopped coming back for lost coats, umbrellas, wallets, car keys, missals, diaries, saccharines, and rosaries, you can put your feet up, and pat yourself on the back.

Greetings that say 'sorry'

This year I am going to send out a lot of Christmas cards to my Christian friends. I don't normally send out either Christmas cards (or Jewish New Year cards) as, no matter how many I send out, I always leave somebody out and make an enemy for life, which is not the point of the exercise.

But this year, I feel I must, because it's been such a messy year for me. There have been so many misunderstandings and jangled feelings and bits of hurt pride that it is the least embarrassing way of saying, 'Sorry, let's make it up', without actually having to mouth the awkward words.

I think every so often you need a time to settle your spiritual account, before the account gets so huge you can't deal with it any more.

At all great religious festivals, even if they are not our own, a longing arises in us for wholeness and for growth; to clamber over the divisions we have so stupidly erected, and go out to meet other people.

We suddenly realize what freedom is. It isn't winning the pools, it's freeing ourselves to unfreeze and smile and send Christmas cards to old friends who might be sore at us. You might feel a bit of a fool and you don't know what the comeback is going to be, but it's worth it.

Sometimes you can't afford expensive presents to go with the card, or indeed any present at all. I have been in that position before and many friends are out of work. But you usually have more to offer them than you think. An old lady in a hospital geriatric ward told me she offers up prayers for friends, because it is the only thing left, and sometimes the only thing left is the greatest.

On a less exalted level, a cooking tip is extremely useful, and this quick avocado sauce has enriched my salads and my reputation. I bless my benefactor – especially as avocados have steadily become cheaper, and are no longer a luxury food but a true democratic delicacy. My benefactor says you should bless God for the fruit and the food processor as it is so easy to make.

Avocado sauce

In a food processor or blender, blend all the ingredients together. Use a teacup as a measure.

½ cup mayonnaise
flesh of 1 large avocado
3 or 4 spring onions chopped
¼ cup cream cheese
¼ cup milk
1 Tablespoon lemon juice
1 clove garlic
1 teaspoon sugar
1 teaspoon salt
¼ teaspoon pepper

This makes a lovely delicate green sauce to put over cooked chicken, fish, or vegetables.

If you use 2 avocados and double the amount of cream cheese, and do not use milk, then you have a pâté which only needs a lettuce leaf as a base, and can be eaten with French bread, cottage loaf, or Jewish Cholla.

Either way it will keep in the fridge for several days.

Re-living the Exodus

When my father went into the army in the First World War, my grandmother was horrified at the thought of my father's eating forbidden food in an army barracks at Passover. So she descended on the camp complete with eleven children, unleavened bread, kosher wine, and two sets of fresh crockery for the festival, one for meat and one for milk. Being a forceful woman, my grandmother got past the sentries, but as she only spoke fragmentary Polish and Yiddish it never became clear to the army authorities quite what she was up to.

At first they thought she was an Irish Republican spy, but no spy could be as flamboyant as my grandma. Eventually, they realized that she was trying to save my father's soul, and his body (or certainly the digestive parts of it) from ritual pollution. This caused great merriment on the barrack square and my father never lived it down.

But this is one thing Jews are meticulous about. On the eve of Passover, all leaven has to be cleared out of the house.

In my home this meant not only ordinary bread, but flour, yeast extract, beer and even rice. We did this to recall, or rather relive, the act of redemption which set off Jewish history with a spanking start.

In the story of the Exodus we are told that the children of Israel left Egypt in such a hurry that they did not have time to let their bread rise. So during the week of Passover we still eat 'the bread of poverty', 'the bread of affliction', the bread of refugees on the run.

You can eat it too. It comes in packets in supermarkets, and tastes like a crisp cheese-biscuit. It is rather fattening; you have to be careful not to eat it endlessly.

The Communion wafer you receive in church is a close relation of the Jewish Matzo bread, and this is not surprising because the Last Supper was a Passover meal, according to Matthew, Mark and Luke, and a pre-Passover meal according to John. Jesus, like Joseph and Mary and all the apostles, and indeed all Jews since the Exodus, celebrated the Passover in an ordinary home accompanied by his friends or family around a supper table.

On that table in front of him there would have been all the symbols which have not changed over the centuries – salt water to represent the Red Sea which the Israelites crossed in safety (and also to represent their tears), four cups of wine because there are four terms for redemption in the Bible account of the Exodus, Charoset (see p. 130) representing the mortar which was used to build the pyramids of Egypt. There are also vegetables to dip in salt water, some say because of ancient hygiene, others because by this dipping the interest of the children is aroused.

The service takes place around the table. The unleavened bread and wine are blessed. A cup of wine is even left for the prophet Elijah, who goes from home to home to sip it. It is odd how a rather short-tempered servant of God has become in tradition the compassionate messenger of the redemption to be.

There are prayers, games, food, nursery rhymes and jokes. But all of them are used, not just to retell the story of the Exodus, but to relive it, and especially to hand on the experience to the children.

So a living tradition is passed on.

When we got to the crossing of the Red Sea, my grandfather used to lead us in procession around the table. We were ancient Israelites, marching out of Egypt, and we carried cushions as luggage. When we reached the edge of the water, my grandfather used to lift up the bottom of his trousers so as not to get them wet.

A friend told me of Passover under the Nazis in Poland during the war, and the strange mixture of foreboding and festival joy. The Last Supper must have had a similar feel to it, for it was probably a Passover meal. There is the dipping in Matthew 26: 23. There are the songs mentioned in Mark 14: 26. I am pretty sure as well that the cup of wine was the cup of Elijah.

These easy little fritters are a Passover domestic delight and the rightful heritage of all children during the festival. They keep all the little ones quiet – and most of the adults too.

Bubeles

Whisk the whites until stiff and fold into the beaten yolks. Mix in the meal and salt. Fry tablespoons in margarine and oil. Turn so that they are golden on both sides. Scatter with sugar.

You can also fry the mixture in a big frying-pan, in which case I suggest you use only 2 eggs and 2 tablespoons meal. Fry on one side, invert with the help of a plate and fry on the other side. Scatter with sugar and cinnamon or serve with butter and honey.

As both eggs and unleavened bread are the symbols of Passover and Easter, I hope the fritters bring the Gospels closer to you.

3 eggs, separated into whites and yolks
3 Tablespoons fine Matzo meal (a kind of cracker crumb made from unleavened bread and available in most cities)
a pinch of salt
margarine, oil
sugar
variation:
butter
honey
cinnamon

Recycling

Thank God the high tide of Chanukah, Christmas, and New Year consumerism is over, and normal caution about money and indigestion has returned. We sort through our loot wondering what on earth we can do with a lot of it, and what we can do with our guilt.

136

What do I do with the three beautiful diaries that have been given me? One diary is useful, two spell danger, and three make a chaos of unkept appointments and untransferred entries. Dare I rub out the inscriptions in two of them, and recycle them? With diaries you have to move fast, so you still remember who gave them to you in the first place. But what about more durable objects? Should one abandon all shame, and attach neat labels, so that you never give people back their own presents?

It happened to me once, but what really annoyed me was that I got back my own present in my own original wrapping paper. I have brooded over this for many years.

Anyway, how long do soaps continue to smell, and what is the shelf life of shaving-cream?

One priest I know gets so many fruit cakes that he comes out in spots. But he is holier than me, and probably than thou as well, so he isn't into recycling.

Some donors are not only generous but saintly. They carefully leave off all inscriptions, and just slip in a card with their name. You can then return the book or record or sell it at a mart or remainder shop.

I can't pretend it's nice or ethical, but what do you do with three copies of last year's pops. Would Mother Teresa want them? Or someone in the Third World, even if you knew where to find it? But these matters are too high for me, as the Psalms and the Book of Job both point out, so I shall return to recycling food.

Recycled sweet and savoury

To hash or not to hash is a delicate question for a delicate tummy.

The best thing to do with Christmas cake is fry it – thick slices of it. It is substantial enough to take it. Serve it hot with any chilled rum or brandy butter left over.

If all the cakes are in bits and impossible to reassemble, then carry on the demolition job till you have a mound of crumbs. Soak them in an egg custard (2 to 3 eggs for a pint of milk sweetened with a little sugar) for at least an hour. Then bake as you would a bread pudding. The result is stodgy but acceptable.

Broken biscuits – digestives, ginger snaps, macaroons etc. can be used as a good base for cheesecake which needs something firm to support it. Also if you mix the crumbs with melted chocolate, nuts and glacé cherries, you can make biscuits out of biscuits. Is it worth it

I ask myself? And I tell myself firmly – no! There are always birds in the garden.

As to poultry bits, I would give them a Mexican flavour. It's strong enough, like charity, to cover quite a lot. This is a Mexican Casserole (sort of) which is intriguing and easy on the cook.

Mexican chicken casserole

In the oil fry the chopped onion, chili and garlic, till the onion is transparent. Add the tomato purée, and a pinch of sugar, and fry 2 or 3 minutes longer. Now add the cummin, oregano, stir, and add the poultry bits. Fry again, and then add the tinned kidney beans (do not use raw beans), and chopped tomatoes. Season. If you want to be more adventurous add a ¼ cup sweet black coffee. Add any cooked peas you have left over, and cook for half an hour. Serve with rice and noodles.

Reheated meat really has to be cooked properly – don't just warm it up or you will have Bacteria Bouillabaise. If you are going to reheat frozen meat consult a book on frozen foods. It's a lesson which has to be studied and learnt.

Serves 4–6
1lb boneless cooked chicken leftovers
3 Tablespoons oil
1 medium onion, chopped
½ chili, deseeded and chopped
1 clove garlic
3 Tablespoons tomato purée
1 teaspoon cummin
1 teaspoon oregano
1 large tin kidney beans (14oz)
1 large tin chopped tomatoes (14oz)
¼ cup sweet black coffee (optional)
cooked peas (optional)
pepper, salt, sugar

Recovery Champagne

One of the nicest things about parties is pottering about among the remains next morning after all the guests have gone. I descend in awful majesty clothed in a dressing-gown and nausea with my new squeaky slippers (a present). I sit for a moment contemplating the ruins, like Edward Gibbon in the Roman Forum, when he decided to write his *Decline and Fall*.

I turn on the Third Programme and mix myself a glass of 'Recovery Champagne' – digestive salts made festive with orange and sweetened lemon-juice instead of water.

The magpie instinct in me asserts itself, and I start rummaging for 'lost and found'. There are predictable lighters (disposable), the keys and the diaries. I stick them by the telephone, for the panic calls which will soon begin.

But what about one rugger sock, a false fingernail, and an interesting letter which begins promisingly: 'How could you!! . . .' Reluctantly but virtuously I put the letter aside, and think about food.

I contemplate it without a shudder because I myself do not intend to eat anything except fruit to clear my system of all the gas and the grease.

There are a lot of things you can do with poultry remains.

Remaindered moussaka

Fry some onions with chopped smoked meat. When the onions are brown, add soy sauce, tomato purée and poultry remains. Stir and mix this hash.

In a greased baking dish put a layer of sliced courgettes, then a layer of hash, then another layer of sliced courgettes, then a layer of sliced fried aubergines. Top this with a thick layer of thin sliced raw potatoes. Season each layer, and fill with stock up to but not including the potatoes. Cover with margarined foil. Bake for 1¼ hrs at 325°F Gas 3 160°C. For the last 30 minutes take off the lid.

Measurements would be silly for a dish like this. Don't be a perfectionist, don't worry, it's not that sort of cooking. Just let yourself go!

onions
smoked sausage
soy sauce
tomato purée
poultry remains
courgettes
aubergine
potatoes
pepper, salt
stock
margarine

You can call it Day After Shepherd's Pie or Remaindered Moussaka, if you have the nerve.

As I wash up the glasses I play a game, and try to work out who drank what from the different colours of the lipstick stains on the glasses. I start to put two and two together and make up numbers which are as fascinating as they are uncharitable.

Regretfully I lay them aside, plunge my hands into the washing-up water and bless the Lord, bawling out fractured bits of my favourite hymns and songs.

'Should ole acquaintance be forgot tum ti tum – ole acquaintance tum ti tum. Good ole acquaintance!'

AWFUL DELIGHTS

I used to have a congregation on the continent. Before I returned to England they invited me to dinner parties. Rare wines were produced and I enjoyed sniffing, considering and gurgling as well as holding them up to the light and testing them for glow. When the dinner party was over, I would hop it smartly to the second-class cross-channel train. On the boat with memories of past grandeur I commanded wine. 'Wadja want luv?' sang out the waitress. 'Red or white, sweet or sour?' It was a refreshing reminder that we were back in Britain.

There are a lot of delights in cooking which are crude; which sound awful but are tasty and comforting. A great gourmet living in England said that British Rail Pork Pies were succulent and meaty. I can't confirm it or deny it, but it goes to show how the good taste of England works strongly in all of us. On stylish Costas, we sigh for Marmite and Brown Sauce. The nicest memories I have of food are eating Captain Kim's fried stew rissoles at sea, or sitting on a pavement in the Mile End Road eating a chip butty with my blood brother.

Awful delights are like Kitsch, which can be first-class if you have the stomach for it. For example I have forgotten the expensive restaurants I was taken to in America, but have never forgotten the 'Strawberry Daiquiri' I was served by a kind family who were determined to give me of their best.

So here they are, delights that the other cookbooks cannot reach – butties, scouse, stew rissoles, and strawberry mush. Enjoy, enjoy.

Sorry, no scouse!

On my way to Liverpool, I read in the newspaper that someone had said it should look to new vistas for trade and profit. The Gardens Exhibition had taken place, and with just a little bit of effort Liverpool had a great future as a centre for tourism and leisure. Perhaps they would have trendy bullfights in New Brighton with a plastic Bull, and a 'horse' inhabited by two comics from the panto.

But I don't think I like Liverpool because I see it as a grisly greyer Costa, or as a grubby Reno or Las Vegas. I like it for itself – just as it is, and I hope they don't litter the side of the Mersey with carriage-lamps in the doorways, and concrete Davids in the backyard 'patios'.

I like the junk shops and the church bazaars and bring and buy sales. It seems to me that Liverpool is quite fully employed in a strange economic cycle.

One half of the town is manufacturing junk and throwing it out, while the other half fight each other in the sales to buy it back. The fights are merry enough, and apart from a few umbrella wounds I'm game for the next scrum.

I also like the look of Liverpool. I think it reminds me most of Dublin, before they struck oil with dairy products, and the whole city got cleaned up.

I am also enchanted by the twang of spoken Scouse, the rhetorical questions which end each sentence, the teasing Welsh and Irish sing-song in it, and the pointed acid humour which pricks all pretension.

I thought of all these things as I sat in the bar of the Adelphi, and happily contemplated the faded glory and the grandeur that remains.

Some of the travel agencies are advertising tourist packages to Siberia, Lapland, Benidorm and Wigan. Give me Liverpool every time.

Scouse is the name of Liverpool's dialect and delicacy, though it is not exactly delicate but convenient. It is a dish dictated by poverty and is starkly simple.

Cut up any cheap bits of meat and put in a saucepan. Cut up any vegetables you can get and add them. Fill the saucepan with water and simmer. Add more water and potato according to need.

Nevertheless I make a sort of Scouse when I don't want to flour, fry or marinade anything. When I'm pooped, and don't want to go out

142

shopping I just put a pot in the oven, and sit back with a drink and the radio.

This is not *the* recipe, but a derivation of it which I made when I put this book together, and the kitchen was awash with paper.

Scouse de luxe, and blind

In a casserole with a lid I put these ingredients, all of which were to hand.

In the oven I bring it to a simmer, and then turn down the heat to 225°F Gas ¼ 110°C. After 3 hours it is ready, the ingredients are soft, and the gravy is delicious. If I had some new potatoes I would put them in too, or also some butter beans.

Anyway over to you, and don't worry about it. Most combinations taste nice if they are left alone to cook long and slowly enough.

If you can't afford any meat at all, it is called Blind scouse.

Serves 4
¾lb steak and kidney, cut
   into small pieces
4 carrots, sliced
½ swede, sliced
1 large parsnip, sliced
2 onions, sliced
1 clove of garlic
flat lager almost to cover
   (real scouse uses water)
1 dessert spoon brown sugar
2 teaspoons salt
2 cloves
1 Tablespoon tomato
   ketchup
1 teaspoon dried mustard
½ teaspoon sage

Heaven on the Central Line

At times in life, the gates of Heaven open for us, without our doing anything about it. For a moment we seem to see things as they really are, and a wave of joy mixed with pain floods into us. With most of us it doesn't last that long, and we can't hold it. A transistor radio blares out, the children scream, and it's gone. But in a way it hasn't, because once you know something – really know it, not just believe it – it can never go.

A lady told me that it happened to her while she was standing in a queue at Sainsbury's. She had been thinking about the food, and whether it would stretch to feeding the family for the weekend, and suddenly she loved.

She loved the old man pushing in behind her, and the tired young

143

woman at the cash desk, and the anxious dog peering in at the shop, yearning for its owner. Then someone prodded her, and someone else said: 'Move your goods up, please,' – and it went. Well, not quite. She sits on a bench in a square near me sometimes and she thinks about it. She is not a particularly religious woman and doesn't quite know what to make of it. But it does her good, she says, and that is precisely what such moments do.

With me it happened in a crowded tube train. I was standing up, swaying on a strap, pushed and pommelled. It felt like a cattle truck, and all of us were beasts – of the nastier sort since cattle are, in fact, rather gentler than humans. Then, for a moment, we weren't a herd of animals rushing along the Central Line, but a coachload of souls, a party of pilgrims travelling to eternity, going home – to our everlasting home.

I was shot out at the next station. Someone trod on my toe. Instead of a nasty remark, I smiled and both of us burst into laughter.

The gates of bliss, if not of heaven also, open for me in a different way when I eat this childhood favourite.

Chocolate bananas

Peel the bananas. Melt the Bournville, and heat with a small knob of butter, the liqueur (because I am now an adult, though with childish tastes) and water. The butter makes the sauce glossy, and the water makes it easy to pour.

Pour the sauce over the bananas, coating them. Put them in a fridge for the chocolate to firm up. Eat them with whipped cream. Even without whipped cream, they are lovely on the Central Line.

You can slice the bananas horizontally and vertically and sandwich them with jam, before you give them chocolate overcoats. But then they are difficult to handle and too rich for my godchild and even for me!

Serves 6
6 bananas
½lb bar of Bournville chocolate
1 knob butter
2 Tablespoons water
1 glass liqueur

Friends drop in for a dip

I was studying at theological college and the text said: 'Go, get thyself a friend!' Another text said somewhat enigmatically that 'Thy friend has a friend'. You understand what it is all about on a public holiday when all the friends, the ones you know and the ones you have never heard of, pay a friendly call on you.

Have a stiff drink, and thank God you've got a little time to transform a party around the table into a bold, bad buffet.

Since you don't know if your friends' friends have friends themselves (someone must love them), the food has to be extended. Dips are a good idea. They are easy, and they give you time to recover and think about what you are going to do next. You can also make them in all sorts of colours, but don't overdo it or the effect will look bilious.

Chips and dips

I use curd cheese or cream cheese as a basis, thinned down to thick cream consistency with yoghourt, and a little milk or mayonnaise.

Now the fun begins. Add a spoon of curry powder with a pinch of ginger and chopped sweet pickle and you will get lovely golden yellow. If it isn't very golden, add some turmeric.

Stir some drained chopped cooked spinach and a pinch of nutmeg into another bowl, and you will have a tender green.

Add some tomato purée, salad cream and mashed tuna and it turns a tempting pink. You can get an even nicer pink by blending together smoked cod's roe, a little chopped onion, garlic, lemon juice and a pinch of sugar, with the dip base.

The changes are endless except for blue (Blue Cheese?). It's a bit of a puzzle, but there isn't much blue in the things we eat.

If you haven't got time for these concoctions, then just crush and sprinkle a packet of onion soup mix into the cream-cheese mixture.

All dips improve if you let them rest and mature – but then so do you!

Now, what do you dip? (People use their hands and it saves washing up.) Anything and everything, except of course your fingers. Little biscuits are fine, so are crisp carrot sticks, cauliflower florets, radishes, celery chunks, and pear and apple slices (sprinkle these with lemon juice first).

If you are determined and brazen, it is a fine time to empty out all the remnants in your pantry.

The result will still look pretty and they were only your friends' friends after all, weren't they? . . . not friends . . . real friends . . . you know what I mean!

But whoever they are, if they have been on a round of parties, they may just want stodge and grease to soak up the alcohol. In which case I recommend Mile End Butties. I used to eat them with my crony on the pavements of Whitechapel in Stepney, when I was a kid. You can make them easily in quantity with the frozen chips for baking.

Mile End butties

Use good quality white bread and butter to make sandwiches. On one side spread the butter with a thin layer of salad cream (not mayonnaise this time). Pile on the chips, salt, and a few drops of vinegar. Add a few potato crisps for crunchiness, and complete the sandwich with its companion slice.

I was told by a friend about an awful delight from up North, Connie Onnie Butties. They were sandwiches filled with sweetened condensed milk. Delicious!

Falling fast out of love

Having read my advice on love potions (Liver and Lovers) and my comments on falling in love, I have been asked to comment on how to end that unhappy state, and fall out of it at the fastest speed you can muster.

Let's face it, though we want love, when we get it, we know it will certainly be quite uncomfortable, possibly quite nasty, and the telephone bill will go up. As we get moody and morose (did he mean? . . . does she really? . . .) we will drop things. Some things don't matter like salt, turnips and empty saucepans. Others do, like eggs, champagne glasses and frying-pans of hot oil. In fact I wouldn't fry if I were you, until you are out of it.

It is dangerous to get lit up without, as well as within, and in any case you are probably on a diet, and sucking your tummy in (don't worry, he or she is too, with the same or another bit of the old anatomy).

Alas, when you're in love, your diary gets into such a muddle.

But how to fall out of it? Well, first, remember all the pleasures you had to forgo, or felt you had to, to get into it – regular hours, nice normal-size feelings, no heavy breathing, and starch.

Very few people ever believe that people will love them as they are, but only as they want them to be, and they apply this to God too, which is very wrong. So they give up all the nice things in life like pastries, for that angular look, which is thought to be desirable.

It is a nice thought when the end is in sight that on the other side of the tears and the renunciation you can make something really sweet with an extra portion of whipped cream, and let out your belt.

Strawberry daiquiris

I first had this 'cocktail' in America as a prelude to a meal of six courses. Being a snob, I tittered to friends about it. Actually I enjoy it, and it is most suitable for post-amorous depression, when a little self-love is needed, because no one else is going to give it to you.

In a blender liquidize the ingredients.

Add castor sugar to taste.

Serve in champagne glasses with ice cubes.

Serves 4 ordinary people, or half that number who are falling out of love
2 bananas
¼lb hulled strawberries
½ cup lime-juice cordial
½ cup orange juice
¼ pint single cream
½ cup Cointreau, Triple Sec or from that strange bottle, brewed by monks (may God forgive them!), you brought back from your holiday
castor sugar to taste

Keep smiling!

Many years ago, I went to America on a lecture tour and fell in love with the place.

I liked Americans. They were more decorative than Europeans, and their language more pithy. They were great dresser-uppers.

147

In the morning, the ladies wore gingham and looked cute and homely over their waffle irons.

In the evening, the same ladies poured themselves into slinky black dresses with startling jewellery. The men often changed from swimming costumes into the hairiest tweeds and the heaviest brogues. (How did they get the strength to lift their feet up?)

I think this was a compliment to me, and I liked meeting Anglo-Scottish lairds in drug stores.

Unfortunately, it was not a question of one smiling hostess, but one hostess after another. When I could only distinguish the smiles, I decided to stop lecturing and get back to unheated, draughty England.

One thing that impressed me about all these kind ladies was their ingenuity and courage. Without hesitation, they mixed pineapple juice, chilis and peanut butter – and *voilà* steak sauce! They laced tinned soups with double tots of alcohol and cream, so that after a bowl or two I could no longer see straight. Having nothing in the cupboard didn't worry them, they used imagination.

They used to make such dramatic events out of ice-cream sundaes. They would clothe the ice-cream in sauce, cream, fruit salad, and nuts. Then on top they would put a marshmallow, and in the marshmallow was a sugar cube soaked in heated gin, which was lit quickly. (No, this was not a children's teaparty, it was for adults only late at night.) Each guest would light his sugar cube, and it would burn very prettily, toasting the marshmallows. Flaring things at table can be a hazard, so you and your guests should be careful. You don't want any burnt sacrifices. I have to admit that I could never light mine. There must have been some trick with it I didn't know.

Americana

I once had the following. It contained tomato juice, concentrated undiluted consommé and vodka in equal parts seasoned with salt and cayenne pepper. It was called a bloodshot.

As I passed out, I have not the slightest memory of its taste or proportions. But (I am told) my face wore a terrible grin, rather like an awful parody of the smile on the face of my kind hostess.

The gourmet afloat

When I used to go sailing, what I lacked in talent I made up in enthusiasm. At an early age I managed to grasp the concept of right and left (right and wrong was easier, which is why I ended up in theology, not the merchant navy). But port and starboard made me insecure and windward and leeward, added to those terms, brought my mind to a standstill and I could only gibber at the tiller.

Changing sails at sea was rather like changing curtains while perched on a shaky chair, and I got so enfolded in them, I nearly got bagged as well, and had to be untwined. To add to this sorry list I could not tie a knot. I have little sense of direction, and no sense of balance.

But some talents I did come up with. I did dive underneath a boat, and tried to free a propeller, knowing well that if the engine was inadvertently turned on I should end up as *rabbin haché* or – more crudely – human hamburger.

I could also translate, somewhat imaginatively, foreign weather forecasts, and above all I could stew anything on the high seas without being sick and, though I myself lived on bananas, could wash up without heaving. This last talent was regarded as a singular grace, and I was justified by it throughout my sailing career.

The thing I enjoyed about sailing was the beauty of it. I never expected the strange phosphorescence which surrounds a boat and makes it magic, or the exhilaration which comes from feeling part of the great surge of wind and tide. And the nights even in the North Sea were magical with stars and distant lights.

I remember a race on a blazingly hot day when the crew reached to the beer-cans only to find they were not self-opening – and there were no openers on board. There was a richness in the language which comes from good Saxon and Norse traditions.

I used to make a simple rough and ready pâté for use in port. It was too rich for making passage. But it did nicely with some French loaf in Ostend harbour, and to my surprise I was complimented by an English lord and an exacting French housewife.

Sludge pâté

Take a large frying-pan, and melt in it the margarine. Add the smoked meat, chopped onions, 3 cloves of garlic, mixed herbs, sliced ox liver, and such extra flavourings as you like, such as anchovy essence, a few juniper or allspice berries, a blade of mace.

When both meats are cooked through, take the pan off the heat, and add the sherry or port. Now mince the entire contents, or even better blend them in a processor.

You will have a nasty brown sludge. Adjust seasonings and salt. Pour the sludge into an earthenware pâté pot to give it that country look. When it is cold, press some orange slices in the top and cover with condensed consommé. This will firm up in the fridge, and is a poor man's aspic. You can also cover it with a layer of melted margarine.

Serves 12 as a starter, 15 as a party dish
½lb margarine
½lb smoked meat
1lb onions, chopped
3 cloves garlic
1 heaped teaspoon mixed herbs
1½lbs ox liver
1 teaspoon anchovy essence (optional)
juniper or allspice berries (optional)
mace (optional)
2 Tablespoons sherry or port (or more if available)
salt, pepper
1 orange
1 tin condensed consommé

Though gourmands shout, and gourmets sneer, it really is quite good, and much better than it sounds. Garbage Soup also sounds dreadful, but is remarkably good. But I think this is enough awful cooking for the moment. I have to guard my reputation.

BAKING

When I am 'old and grey and full of sleep' I shall take up baking and contemplation. Both share a deep slow rhythm, and a purifying odour. I shall make cakes with a theological message, such as Angel Cake and Devil's Food Cake, and decorating biscuits will be an innocent pastime when passion is not the problem it was.

Until I reach that placid plateau, I stick to a few easy recipes which I don't need to look up. There are of course special problems from the Law of Moses. At Passover for example, yeast is out, so cakes have to be propped up by egg whites and faith.

I think to bake properly, you need children who have a deep respect for cakey smells and biscuit colours, and who are both critical and encouraging. I don't have any – to my regret.

To love, honour
& learn to
BAKE
properly..

151

What's missing

We were at a meeting discussing spirituality.

'Cookery books', said my neighbour, 'and recipes', she added, 'are always too complicated, and they never give the whole story'. She was right, and you have to know how to read a recipe as well as cook it.

I remembered all the disasters of my culinary career. When I started I was quite ambitious. Instead of learning how to jug a kipper or boil an egg, I decided to make rich shortcrust pastry. The ingredients were right, so were the measurements, and I did everything I was supposed to do. I checked through the recipe three times. I sat back and thought I was going mad.

Every time I rolled the 'thing' out, more chunks got glued on to the rolling-pin, and what was left looked like my grandmother's Nottingham lace doilies. The book said it was a cookery book, but perhaps it was really about origami instead? I threw away the rolling-pin, and tackled the object with my bare fists.

There were now more holes than ever, and for the first time in my life I literally wrung my hands. (You read about this action in novels but how often do you ever see it!) The dough got greyer and greyer as my fists got whiter and whiter. Finally with great deliberation, I opened the window, and hurled my shortcrust through it. At least that is what I tried to do. One lump stuck to my hands, another fell neatly into the sink, and another hit my dog Re'ach, who sat on her haunches and howled.

At the bar that night, I told my tale. 'You chump,' they said, 'what about the flour?'

'I used enough flour in it,' I said, 'and it was the best quality.'

They explained carefully, as people explain to a backward child, that you have to flour the board and flour the rolling-pin as well. The book just never mentioned that.

Some books on spirituality are like that too. They give you a lovely recipe for holiness and it all seems very clear, until you try to practise it. But something obvious gets left out – like human nature.

A friend of mine gave me a recipe for Turkish Delight Slices. To be honest I have simplified it by using bought pastry. But if you like Turkish Delight in quantity, it works well enough.

Turkish (or Greek) delight slices

Roll out a packet of sweet rich shortcrust (I cheat and use frozen) into a long rectangle (12″ × 4″). Cut the Turkish delight pieces into long strips and arrange them on the pastry in a line parallel to the long edge of the pastry.

Roll up the pastry and cut into slices (1½″). Put them on a greased baking tray and bake for half an hour in a moderate oven (350°F Gas 4 180°C).

Sprinkle generously with icing sugar.

1lb shortcrust pastry
6oz Turkish delight
icing sugar

Two left feet

I remember as a child looking at my vest in a completely bewildered way, wondering what bit of me fitted into which hole. It seemed so complicated that after swimming lessons I left off all my underclothes and went home in a mac where I could sort it all out. Some people have the knack for that sort of thing.

I have a terrifying relation (aged six) who not only takes plugs apart, but also puts them together. He repairs fuses, transistors, and has begun to computerize his spending patterns. Unlike me he never strangled himself by trying to push his head through an armhole.

I have always admired such competence wistfully. I have a friend who talks to recalcitrant motors firmly and slaps them. For him they work. I have other friends who can peel, segment and eat oranges daintily at a formal dinner party, without wallowing in their juice, or spraying it over others. There are others yet, who can get their peas to their mouth without gluing them to the fork with mashed potato.

For all such people I give thanks. But sometimes the incompetent, and the clumsy, and those who didn't quite make it have something very special to offer.

This is a cheesecake even a clumsy person like me can make – It doesn't require laboratory accuracy in measurements, and it doesn't collapse when you open the oven door.

Clumsy Rabbi's cherry and almond cheesecake

Serves 8
About 10 digestive biscuits
2 eggs
¼lb castor sugar
½lb curd cheese
½lb cream cheese
a few drops of vanilla
3oz glacé cherries halved
2oz flaked almonds

Crush the biscuits and put them in the bottom of a loose-bottomed or spring-form cake tin. Beat the eggs with the cheeses, sugar and vanilla essence. Mix in the cherries. Pour the mixture over the digestive biscuits. Cover the top with flaked almonds.

Bake in a moderate oven (350°F Gas 4 180°C) for 45 to 60 minutes. Leave in the baking dish overnight in the fridge to firm up.

I like almost saints, mystics who never quite manage to take off, and visionaries who need bifocals.

I went to a talk on English mystics. I felt suitable reverence for Julian of Norwich and Walter Hilton, and Richard Rolle, of course, but my heart warmed really to Margery Kempe. How irritating she must have been, and how tiresome.

I imagine her trudging towards Prussia (what an extraordinary place for a 14th-century pilgrimage – unpackaged by even mediaeval standards), abandoned in Venice, and imprisoned in England. No one is ever going to canonize her though she was very devout, because she was always putting her big foot in it. But in my prayers I sometimes think of her, and her clumsy big feet, and it helps me.

I find a gem

Some friends asked me to recommend them a restaurant. What sort did they want, I asked, and what did they want to eat? They explained their needs and, like everybody else, they wanted a portion of pie-in-the-sky in a castle-in-Spain. The restaurant they wanted should be cheap – not cheap-cheap, but chic-cheap. The cooking should be unaffected, with a simple menu of unpretentious bisques, soufflés and bavaroises, just the sort of thing any country cook knocks up for elevenses. The establishment should be mentioned in the *Good Food Guide*, and be undiscovered. (How then was I to know about it?) It should also be off the beaten track, and accessible by car.

I informed them that like the Isles of the Blest such restaurants are hidden from human gaze. In gastronomic as in spiritual matters you usually get what you pay for, and the quality gets higher with the price.

There are, of course, exceptions, but it's best not to bank on them. There are moments of grace in the dreariest spiritual deserts, unexpected, unmerited and unsettling. There are wonderful moments of good eating where all you ever hoped for was a sawdust hamburger embalmed in a bun.

And talking of embalming, one of the nicest places I know is a café in a crematorium. I found it by accident, after taking three services one after the other. I was looking rather white, and a kindly undertaker led me to a door in a quiet corner. I stumbled through it and found myself in a gentle, comfortable restaurant. There were little tables, and chintz cushions, and kindly ladies behind the counter. It was like a throwback to the genteel tea places I was taken to as a child, where we had a pot of tea for two (India or China, milk or lemon, and another jug of hot water, waitress . . . 'Don't play with the sugar-tongs, child' . . .) served with a plate of assorted pastries and toasted tea-cakes.

It was so comforting, and I ordered all the things I hadn't eaten for years. As I munched Eccles cakes and toasted buns, death seemed less hostile and more friendly. Once again I marvelled how affection and tranquillity can transform all things.

Now, do I recommend this gem to my friends? It is undiscovered but accessible. It is inexpensive, and the food is jolly good. As far as I am concerned it is the *crème de la crème*. It is the only truly undiscovered place I know.

I like having a dainty tea with such pre-war delights as a strainer, a slop bowl, and a teapot and jug all for yourself. With the tea, I eat generous slices of fruit cake.

Up North the standard of baking is higher than the effete South. This simple recipe for a fruit cake can be made by anybody who can find a jar of mincemeat. I came upon this recipe in a journal of the Wardle Community Association, and I was kindly allowed to pass it on. It's a no problem cake

Mincemeat fruit cake

Cream the margarine and sugar. Whisk in the eggs and add the rest of the ingredients. Mix well. Turn into an 8-inch cake-tin lined with greaseproof paper. Sprinkle with flaked almonds. Bake for 1¾hrs at 325°F Gas 3 160°C.

½lb self-raising flour
5oz castor sugar
5oz soft margarine
3 eggs (size 3)
1lb jar mincemeat
chopped glacé cherries, chopped walnuts and sultanas (about 6oz in all)
1oz flaked almonds for topping

Cake and kindness

My secretary and I work in a small crowded room. We share it with two cacti, four phones, five filing cabinets, and unsteady towers of reference books. There are postcards on the walls, and a teddy bear which appeared quite mysteriously and has never been moved. Photos and mementos of holidays are scattered around: an alabaster ash-tray from Stresa, a miniature canal boat, and a mug from Cornwall.

If you are a rabbi, minister, or priest, people often ring you up if they are in trouble, not if things are going well. So though our four phones ring constantly, the tidings are not that joyful, and there is a lot of muddle, and sadness, and confusion as people ask us to sort out an ecclesiastical jam.

In life there are often no answers or at least no obvious ones. People just have to learn to live with their problems, just as we all live with aging and death. All you can do is show concern and kindness. My secretary shows this. She also does more. When people call in person she gives them coffee and cake if she has time. This is her 'ministry', for giving cake is a kindness, and kindness is another word for religion.

I can't make cake like my secretary and I only succeed with very easy ones like this. You don't have to sift anything, and can beat all the ingredients together in one bowl. Also the proportions are so easy to remember. I don't have to look up the recipe. That's why I call it:

666,333 chocolate coffee cake (with 4411 filling)

6oz self-raising flour
6oz soft margarine
6oz castor sugar
3oz drinking chocolate
3 eggs (size 3)
3 Tablespoons hot strong instant coffee

Filling:
4oz soft margarine
4oz icing sugar
1 dessert spoon drinking chocolate
1 dessert spoon dry instant coffee powder

Mix all the cake ingredients together slowly. Grease and fill two 7-inch cake tins. Bake on the middle shelf of the oven at 350°F Gas 4 180°C for 35 minutes.

For the filling, mix all ingredients together and stir till smooth with a wooden spoon. Use it to sandwich the 2 cakes.

It's very toothsome but don't eat it all yourself, give a slice to someone who needs it. My secretary does.

Cooking it right, chapter and verse

I am always behind in answering letters so I refer all my patient correspondents to their Bibles and cite Habakuk 2: 3. Some of the letters are about cooking measures, metric, American, Imperial, and commonsense. For the last, I use a measuring cone. For sentiment, I use a small, old biscuit-tin, the lid of same, a small vase intended for roses, which has glass bobbles going up the side at convenient and regular intervals, a teacup without a handle, and a mug. I also use a broken knife and a tin-opener I bought many years ago in East Berlin which nips everybody else, but is quite docile with me.

Now I can't say add a biscuit-tin lid of water to the dough and stir with two-thirds of a knife, though that is the truth of the matter.

Some of the letters raise fascinating points. One enquiry was about that strange word *Selah* which pops up mysteriously in the middle of the psalms, replacing our piety with a puzzle. Well, it's like my cooking measures, very difficult to be exact about. Some people say it means you should fall flat and knock your head on the ground. Others say it's nothing to do with you at all, just an instruction for the choirmaster – though they cannily don't give the instruction away. Others say that it was what King David said when one of his harpstrings broke!

Some letters have given me extraordinarily good hints for cooking. But I do have to say that Black Pudding is out for a variety of reasons, theological and otherwise. So attempts to serve it in a sauce are interesting but theoretical.

I also get shaken by the simple but direct quality of some questions, for example, 'What must Jews believe?' To be honest I am really not sure, because there is no equivalent to the Creed in Judaism.

One enquirer asked about Oblaten – a rather extraordinary cake made out of wafers, which comes from Central Europe.

My friend Eve, who lived in Scotland but whose mother came from Austria and whose father came from Czechoslovakia tells me you make it like this.

Oblaten torte (Wafer cake)

Buy a packet of circular Oblaten (wafers), sold by most high-class delicatessen stores and in many supermarkets. The wafers now are produced by a number of countries: Austria, Germany, Czechoslovakia, Hungary and Poland. However, historically these hail from Carlsbad – in Czechoslovakia – and were an original recipe handed down from generation to generation. The wafers were traditionally covered with a variety of fillings, before they were assembled and topped with pure chocolate coating and served with a dollop of fresh whipped cream.

Here is my friend's traditional filling which is a Czech one:

Mocha buttercream filling

Mix butter, sugar and almonds together to a smooth paste. Add coffee, chocolate and finally liqueur, mix well. If mixture is too firm a little more liqueur can be added. But the consistency should be firm enough to spread.

Now spread each layer of wafer with the buttercream. The top layer can either be spread with the cream, or for festive occasions, topped with plain melted chocolate.

Heat the chocolate in a saucepan, very gradually, with a little water and a knob of butter (for a glazed effect). When liquid pour it over the entire cake. The cake is better made a few days in advance and stored in a fridge.

You can use fan wafers instead of Oblaten, though the Oblaten are thinner, and more delicate.

Don't forget dollops of cream.

½lb unsalted butter
½lb sugar
2oz ground almonds
2 dessertspoons instant coffee (or to taste)
1 dessertspoon powdered chocolate
1 soupspoon rum or cherry liqueur
2 small bars of Bournville chocolate (optional)

A close encounter

It was most embarrassing. I had come to a retreat on the inner life, but the pressures of my outer and professional life made me late. I did not know the conference centre I was attending, so I hurried through room after room until I saw a group of people sitting in a circle and waiting. I took a chair and joined their circle. I closed my eyes and prepared myself to dive into that great silence out of which a still small voice can speak.

There are qualities of silence. As I meditated I became uneasily aware that something was wrong. Nobody made a noise or disturbed the gathering, but even with my eyes closed, I began to feel no companionship or support from my fellow retreatants (which I was used to) but suspicion and even hostility. I told myself I was imagining things and concentrated harder. It was no use.

Then a voice broke in. 'I want to say something,' it said. I waited for a prayerful word. The voice continued, 'I think we should throw him out.' He meant me!

Now I have been bounced out of a student meeting, and refused membership of a vegetarian group, because I was seen with a sausage, but I had never been blackballed from On High. My jaw dropped as a heated argument then developed as to whether I could be tolerated (!) or sent back to where I had come from (?).

I made a timorous suggestion that we should pray about it, but this turned on the heat appallingly. It was a real rave-up, in which any still small voice required a disc-jockey's amplifier.

Eventually all was revealed. There were two conferences at the centre. One was a retreat and the other a meeting of encounter groups, eager to come clean about hostility. The groups sent delegates to each other. Being late I had wandered into the wrong world.

Later on in the bar our jangled feelings were soothed. There was even a recognition that unexpected encounters can be providential.

Religious people are often cowards about the expression of their own aggression. They do not transform it, they just suppress it. Counselling, therapy and encounter groups are not aware enough of the healing in prayer, and the help that comes from an invisible source if you invoke it, and listen to it as well as speaking to it.

This chocolate roll puts everybody in a good temper.

Judith Smith's chocolate roll

Whisk the egg whites until they are stiff. Add the sugar, 1 Tablespoon at a time. Fold in the yolks, then the sifted cocoa. Whisk briefly to mix it all. Pour on to a generously greased grease-proof paper, lining a swiss-roll tin. Bake in a very hot oven (450°F Gas 8 230°C) for 9 to 10 minutes. Take it out of the oven, and turn it on to a tea-towel. Separate the cake immediately from the paper (carefully using a knife). Place the paper back on the cake and roll with the tea-towel on the bottom and the paper on top. The paper will not stick any longer but will keep the delicate Swiss roll together. This cake usually stays in one piece and doesn't crack.

Cool rolled for 2 hours. Then open carefully, remove the paper, and spread with the whipped filling. Roll up again.

Serves 4

4 eggs (size 3) separated
3 Tablespoons castor sugar
2 Tablespoons sifted cocoa (the sifting is important)
Filling:
5oz whipping cream whipped with 2 Tablespoons of castor sugar

Eating in bed

Some people really like it! They balance bowls of cornflakes on their knees and hide dishes of scrambled eggs and kidneys among the blankets. Some keep a packet of Muesli and a pint of milk on the bedside table in case they suffer from night starvation and need a snack at 4 o'clock (a.m., not p.m.).

I just can't do it. The mechanics of it are so appalling. I would have to be in the best of health to mastermind the operation. The only occasion it ever arises in my life is when I am ill and not at my brightest or best.

161

Toast crumbs are the worst. Trying to relax on a toast-crumb-scattered sheet is a scratchy and depressing nightmare. Boiling liquids which don't balance come next. I prefer burns to weals, but you may think differently, as we are not made alike. Slithering and slippery things are not a danger to health, but they can lead to acute tension and possible breakdown.

A friend brought me some smoked salmon as a treat – the best type, Scotch and slippery. Most of it got into my mouth, but the telephone rang and one slice slithered away and disappeared in a tangle of sheets. I felt it certainly, but couldn't find it. It was so upsetting, I jumped out of bed and decided to get well instead.

These very delicate cinnamon balls are safe and very comforting. Some of the sugar dust does come off, but it is easily blown away and doesn't make me too itchy. This recipe uses no flour, and is therefore popular with Jews at Passover, whether they are upright or horizontal.

Almond and cinnamon balls

Mix all the ingredients together except the egg whites. Whip the whites till firm and fold in gently. Roll into balls – they will be sticky – and place them on a greased and floured baking tray. Bake for 20 minutes 325°F Gas 3 160°C till golden. Dust them with sugar.

Makes about 15
4oz castor sugar
8oz ground almonds
1½ teaspoons cinnamon
3 egg whites
1 egg yolk

Motivated to pray

I've just taken a retreat for Alcoholics Anonymous, and as is so often the case I got more out of it than I gave. The greatest thing they gave me was helping me to believe again that inner change is possible. Yes, I know I ought to believe it, because I recite prayers about it, and urge it on everybody from the pulpit. But I have to admit, I find it hard-going. Each year at the Jewish New Year and Day of Atonement, I promise I'll be a good boy for the coming year, and I mean it. But a few weeks afterwards, I look at my life and can't really notice any difference. After a number of years it gets you down. I get sceptical about the nice hopeful words in the liturgy.

As I listened to people's stories at the retreat, I began to realize where I was going wrong. Their motivation was so much greater than mine. Some needed a 'Power greater than themselves' to rescue them from the fear of a collapsed liver and convulsions, and a psychiatric ward. So they really prayed, they didn't just dabble with prayers.

The Bible doesn't say all prayers are going to be answered. For as the prophet Jeremiah assures us, you'll find God – if you 'search with all your heart', that is.

On thinking back over my prayers over the last years, I had never done that. I had been hoping the Almighty would bump into me. I had never looked for Him with everything I had got. I had dabbled in religion but I hadn't practised it – I thought I had, but it's very easy to fool yourself.

I was also astounded by their honesty. People didn't hide behind their respectability, they really invited you into the kitchens and bathrooms of their lives as well as the parlours. They were able to give their experience to each other and to me. They also gave me so much food, that I couldn't get into any of my clothes, and only my robes which are cut on ample lines fit me.

But I can't go to the supermarket in black bombazine with a velvet hat and a pom-pom to match. In the hall at the retreat everybody had put a delicacy on the table. There were platters and plates of dried bananas, cheeses, chocolate, cherry almond cake and much more. It was more than flesh and blood could resist.

At the discussions people used to start off by saying, 'I'm so-and-so, and I'm an alcoholic'. Well, I'm Lionel Blue. I could be an alcoholic, but I am certainly a glutton.

A lady at the retreat gave me a recipe for Almond and Cherry Cake. It was delicious and next time I visit them I shall try to bring along my own contribution. This Passover Chocolate Cake would find favour. It's easy to remember the ingredients because you need a ¼lb of nearly everything.

Passover chocolate cake

Serves 8
¼lb butter
¼lb castor sugar
¼lb ground hazelnuts
¼lb plain chocolate
2 teaspoons instant coffee
4 eggs separated into yolks and whites (make sure there is no yolk in the white)
¼ pint whipping cream

Using a processor, grate the chocolate and powder the hazelnuts. Beat the sugar and butter together with the chocolate. Beat in the egg yolks. Mix in the hazelnuts and coffee. Beat the whites till stiff and fold in. Bake in a buttered cake tin for 1 hour at 375°F Gas 5 190°C.

It's very luxurious with whipped cream.

NIBBLES AND BITS

There are many cures for depression and anxiety now available, and nearly all of them are unpleasant. I suggest a comforting supplement which also brings reassurance in difficult times – a well-stocked store cupboard of bits. Pickling and potting are gentle arts, and it is only prudent to lay in some goodies against the wrath which comes into our lives at one time or another.

In Jewish tradition there is a feast stored up for the righteous, in the world to come. Who does the catering is rather obscure, though presumably there is no need for the meal to be under strict ecclesiastical supervision. But as it will be a Jewish-style meal, though not of course restricted to Jews, it must commence with cucumbers, sweet, crisp and pickled.

I like a nice NIBBLE between NIBBLES..

A suitcase philosophy

Having lived out of a suitcase for many years, I have grown philosophical about it. I no longer struggle with it, curse it, or pray about it – I accept its dimensions as they are, submit meekly and live accordingly.

These are my tips on holiday packing, and if you are not a perfectionist they may confirm you in your untidy but reasonable habits.

If you are, on the other hand, a Tissue Paper Wrapper, then please pass over the following and get to the recipe as soon as possible.

Pack three plastic bags – for your dirty smalls, for your clean smalls, and for your dirty but usable smalls. This last saves you on the last few days of the holiday. After you've been oiled and grilled for a week, you feel too woozy for delicacy.

I invested in an anti-mosquito vaporizing machine, and have never suffered since those awful night waves of insect bombers glutted with North European blood. Either that or a good insect repellent – in this case forget about economy, get the best.

The same advice for earplugs. In Venice the alley was narrow and all the windows were open. Three TVs were playing loudly enough to vibrate the furniture and they were all showing different programmes. I used two earplugs in each ear, but I was the only one who slept.

A bottle of Marmite, because as far as I'm concerned its salty taste is forever England, and it's a wonderful antidote to too much 'Eviva España' and all those burnt bits from the barbecues, and with hot water a nice change from cheap brandy.

One or two books of spirituality are necessities not luxuries. Watching the turntable at the airport won't bring your luggage closer, and contemplation comes very easily when your world is awash with vanities. Thoughts about eternity are very suitable in such places as Luton, Gatwick, Heathrow and Stansted. Also remember it is not easy keeping any friendship going for a fortnight abroad and a little detachment will help.

Since it is possible that for part of your holiday you will be marooned in the departure lounge, you will need something to munch. If you eat too many sandwiches and sticky buns you won't get into your holiday slacks or shorts bought optimistically one size too small. Vegetable *crudités* are a good French solution.

In a plastic bag, put quartered, peeled carrots, and thick slices of green peppers, cauliflower florets, slices of apple, chunks of cucumber, raw red cabbage and radishes. I would miss out spring onions and tomatoes. Make sure that all the vegetable bits are washed and carefully dried. You can put the juicier ones in separate little plastic bags.

Fill one plastic pot with a good quality mayonnaise, not salad cream. Stir in a handful of finely-chopped fresh parsley and herbs. You can fill other plastic pots with other dips – salad cream (not mayonnaise) flavoured with a little curry powder and the juice from a mango chutney bottle is a good one, so is commercially-soured cream mixed with chopped chives. The more colours the better – it will keep you all cheerful.

Pass around the vegetables and let everyone dip them into the pots. Plates are not needed, but napkins are, or rather, a sturdy roll of kitchen paper.

Some iced wine in a vacuum flask will provide a taste of the continent before time, and will save you the scrum around the departure lounge bar.

Some great spiritual teachers thought life was rather like a waiting-room. It's certainly not your eternal home, but there is no reason why you shouldn't make yourself as comfortable as you can before you get there.

Every few months I have to attend a clinic at the hospital. At first I resented it. I looked at my watch, and pestered the receptionist. The minutes (and sometimes the hours) went by. I watched people expostulate and walk out. When you are ill you either get very tetchy or very accepting.

I learnt the trick of it from an old lady who used to sit next to me as we waited. Waiting in the waiting-room, she said, was her great treat of the week. She didn't have to work or do anything. There were lots of people there, so she wasn't lonely, and all of them were interesting. There was also a coffee-bar downstairs, but she brought her own provisions, as even hospital coffee-bars are out of reach on an old-age pension. You could, she said, make a treat out of anything if you don't rush it.

On her advice I decided to accept the present moment, and live in it. This isn't as easy as it sounds. So much of our thinking is locked up in fears from the past or hopes for the future that the present moment gets lost. I worried so much about getting out of the hospital that I never explored the possibilities of the waiting-room. I now respect the time I spend there, and like all things treated with respect, it ceases to be a desert but flowers or blossoms (sort of).

The hospital waiting-room has become my cloister. Religiously it is now where I feel most at home. I take a book with me, and it is a wonderful place for spiritual reading. I don't like heavy books, so my favourites are old copies of Mount Carmel and a pamphlet I picked up on St Teresa.

The waiting-room has become my Interior Castle, and when my name is called, it now seems too soon, not too late. I watch the people sitting with me, and the chairs that fill and empty. It is like an image of life itself, and sometimes there is a great bonus. If I am very quiet, it seems to me that one of the empty chairs is empty, yet occupied, for the presence of God occupies it, and waits for us as we wait for the doctor in the waiting-room.

Anyway the waiting-room is now comfortable and comforting. It's nice being with the old lady and the Presence.

Although I can afford the coffee-bar, I recommend this kind of fudge. It's nice to eat yourself and pass around. It's very simple, but not for you if you are on a diet.

I have to point out though that the recipe requires a very large and solid pot (boiling sugar is explosive so be warned), a very sturdy wooden spoon and muscles. The fudge which is called Tablet is therefore best made in the interval between waiting-rooms, when you are fighting fit. The recipe was given to me by Father Gordian Marshall, a Dominican friend, and I am giving his precise instructions.

Tablet

Pour the water into your sturdy pot (to stop the sugar sticking) and then pour all the sugar on top and bring to the boil. When it is boiling, add the butter. When the butter has melted and is beginning to boil too add the tin of condensed milk. Boil briskly for about 45 minutes, stirring regularly to stop it sticking. This is when you will need the muscles God gave you and the big sturdy pot and spoon you yourself provided.

During this time, it will change colour and become reddish brown. When it begins to hold its shape, and before it becomes solid, take it off the heat. As it cools, beat it vigorously with the spoon.

When the texture is slightly granular, pour it into a shallow tin and leave it to set. But before it sets, score it with a knife into the pieces you will require. If you have overcooked it, the fudge will be a little coarse in texture. If you have undercooked it and it won't set, all you have to do is reboil it for a few minutes, and it will be all right.

2¼lb granulated sugar
5oz unsalted butter
1 large tin sweetened
   condensed milk
2 teacups water

Once you get the knack of it, it isn't difficult. It will exercise your muscles and you will be a hit in the high society of the hospital waiting-room.

It has millions of calories, but it will take a lot of weight off your mind.

A Jew among Catholics

I went to Chester to speak to the Newman Society on Jewish–Christian relations. They gave me the warmest of welcomes, and listened attentively while I unburdened myself for nearly an hour of all my inner-self questioning and probing on this subject.

On the way home, I began to consider the quality of their attention, and my own openness. It went beyond the normal politeness of genteel ecumenism and dilettante interest in comparative religion. You know the sort of thing: 'We should like to thank the speaker for his enlightening remarks . . . on Zen Buddhism, or vegetarianism, or palmistry, or whatever.'

We listened to each other because we needed something from each other, but it was a puzzle to work out what it was. It is difficult to see another religious world from within, and to view its questions and its problems according to its own self-understanding and not according to your own misunderstanding.

But I think we are beginning to try, and some new courage came with Vatican II. The Holy Spirit is drawing us to questions which could not be faced before, because in the post-war years there has been a growth in trust between Catholics and Jews. We have begun to invite each other, not just into the parlours and drawing-rooms of our faiths, but into each other's kitchens.

On the Catholic side – I speak as an outsider – it seems to me that there has been a change in emphasis in Catholic piety. Catholics want to see the Holy Family and the disciples not just as icons, but also as the living people they were in the religious world of their time. That world was not the world of the Hebrew scriptures, but the world of early rabbinic Judaism. Mary must have practised the pieties of that Judaism, and Jesus preached in the synagogues, which are never mentioned in the Old Testament and were the creation of that piety. That is why I think Catholics are interested in listening to a rabbi.

In Chester I stayed with the Capuchin Friars, who gave me truly Franciscan hospitality. I pondered on the Catholic religious orders, and their ideals, and their celibate life. Judaism has its own spirituality and holiness, but it has no equivalent to the Capuchin.

A generous couple at the meeting gave me a home-made bottle of Pesto, which is a delicious Italian sauce for all types of pasta. My recipe is more like Salsa Verde.

Here, at least, is the best that I can offer.

In the old days they made it with a mortar and pestle. I suggest you only attempt it if you have a food processor.

Pesto

Blend the ingredients in the food processor.

You can cover the mixture with cling foil and it keeps well in the fridge. I have also used strong Cheddar (though this will make the purists shudder) when I have had no Parmesan. But as I served a dollop of the Pesto on a baked potato, not on pasta (it is like butter), it was a case of one compromise in another.

3 anchovy fillets
2 crushed cloves garlic
2 teaspoons fresh basil (dried will do)
a handful fresh parsley
5 Tablespoons Parmesan cheese
1oz butter
5 Tablespoons olive oil including that from the anchovy tin
2 Tablespoons pine nuts or shelled walnuts
3 Tablespoons lemon juice
2 teaspoons sugar
6 grinds of pepper

It is quite strong and very rich, so you won't need too much of it.

Stop dithering!

For the last week I have been trying to fill out a form. It's not a complicated one, and as a professional bureaucrat I should have finished it off in five minutes. Well, I haven't.

Not that I've wasted my time exactly, because looking at it I have instead drawn a picture of two cows, some railway stations, and something which might have started out as a cathedral, but has turned into a soufflé, and might become a Martian. I think I shall give one of the cows a moustache.

All of us get these hang-ups. With me it's forms, but with others it can be a telephone-call, or a bread-and-butter letter, or a simple reply to an invitation.

With some people it isn't just wasting time on doodles, the problem grows out of all proportion, and ends up as a depression. The trouble is that we confuse being perfect with being perfectionist, which isn't the same thing at all. Here is an example.

A young man came to see me in a terrible dilemma about jobs. He had had two offers (almost indistinguishable), and which should he take? Instead of being delighted with his employment situation, the burden of choice had wrecked his enjoyment. So instead of celebrating, he sat there twitching and smoking and shaking. Which was the right one? he wailed.

Well, in such situations there just isn't a right answer. No job ever fits anybody exactly, and lots of situations can't be worked out in advance, because there are just too many unknown factors. The real victory is to choose either and stick by it, not to get paralysed with doubt. And what if it doesn't turn out right? Well, you can't win all the time, so don't get nasty with yourself or force yourself to answer impossible questions. ('How long is a piece of string?')

You know the sort of situations I'm talking about. You've planned a little supper party. You've got it all worked out and off you go to the supermarket. But when you're there you see that some chocolate-coated broccoli or such is going remarkably cheap, and then you start dithering and changing course and before you know where you are you have bought half the ingredients for one meal and half for another, and they don't combine. ('What, smoked mackerel and chocolate-coated broccoli!')

My advice, and I speak from experience, is don't try to be too clever. Just go back to what you first thought of. Yes, the broccoli was cheap and very unusual certainly, but all the excitement isn't good for your nerves, and valium is getting more expensive even on the National Health.

With a form, it's a good idea to fill in the bits you can and send it off straight away, with a little note on it that you've got stuck and can't do any more.

Quite often it's not your fault at all, and the questions on it are just unanswerable. Being perfect doesn't mean that you have to take responsibility for the universe.

When you've been jangled you need something easy, sweet and toothsome to reduce the drama. Old childhood favourites are very good for shock. Of these the nicest is Cinnamon toast.

Cinnamon toast

Toast slices of wholemeal bread on one side. Mix together the melted butter or margarine, brown sugar, and cinnamon. Spread the mixture on the untoasted side and grill until toffeeish, but sticky.

You don't have to be perfectionist about making it. But in its humble way at the right time, it's perfect.

Serves 6
¼lb melted butter or good-quality margarine
6 Tablespoons brown sugar
1 heaped teaspoon cinnamon
6 slices wholemeal bread

Potted temper, or what to do with remnants

I never know what to do about my remnants. I go to a retreat and feel lovely, but there's always some remnants of temper which never got sorted out and come out at the most surprising moments, shocking my neighbours, and me even more. And then there are all those remnants of string and material and wrapping-paper after Christmas which you can't bear to throw away.

If you were a really good housekeeper, one of those who never has to hunt through the laundry baskets for the socks or stockings you only wore once (well, twice in fact), you would rise to the occasion superbly. You would turn the remnants into toy ducks, pen-wipers (do they still exist?), sachets, egg-warmers, and mothball covers. I don't. I just stuff them into my oblivion drawer. Most fridges have good oblivion areas – those hidden parts at the back, behind the stock bowl. In this 'no-go' area lurk little stumps of dry cheese, expensive Camembert, nifty now with ammonia, and 1½ tablespoons of stew too good to throw away, but what do you do with it?

Now some things you can't do much with and I am not a pen-wiper addict myself. I don't know what you do with remnants of temper except suppress them, and I think you had better do the same with the chemical Camembert.

As for the 1½ tablespoons of stew, gobble it or get rid of it. The cheese stumps are not beyond redemption.

The easy way is to turn them into Welsh Rarebit (softened with hot milk) or grate them and scatter them over hot soup.

But if they are not too far gone and beyond hope, you can transform them into that old English delicacy – Potted Cheese. It is very simple.

Potted cheese

cheese remnants
margarine or butter
cayenne pepper
sherry or port
walnuts
salt
mustard or anchovy essence

Grate, crumble or mash all the cheese remnants you can find which have not gone off (no ammonia please).

Mash them together with about half their weight of softened margarine or butter.

Season with a pinch of cayenne and a shake of the sherry or port remnants (you don't need much). Test for salt.

Flavour with a little mustard or anchovy essence but don't get carried away. Mix in some finely chopped walnuts.

Taste as you go along, and what you don't eat pack into little pots.

Let the mixture amalgamate and firm up in the fridge. Serve in little pots, with a walnut half on top of each. With hot toast or biscuits it's lovely.

174

What you do with your temper remnants I cannot say. You can't pot them like cheese.

How to get potted

Olde-tyme cooking is fun, provided you don't get sentimental about dishes you have never tasted. Roman cooking, for example, has its devotees, though no one is quite sure about ingredients or quantities. Using an olde-tyme cook book is quite an adventure since you have to guess how much you use of anything. 'Season to taste' is the least of it. The Romans seemed to like their dishes sweet and smelly at the same time. They were addicted to a sauce made of honey, spices, meat stock, and rotting fish, and they used it as liberally as the brown-sauce bottle in a 'caff'. As they also over-ate while reclining, propping up their heads on their hands, indigestion must have been rampant.

Strangely enough, modern machinery such as a powerful processor makes a lot of old-tyme dishes possible. Potted beef, made in the days when good steak was cheap and labour even cheaper, is once again on the menu. It is almost as good as any French pâté and much less fatty. The old-tyme books tell you to use old-tyme sirloin with old-tyme spices, but as I can't pay old-tyme pryces, I use shin, the cheapest possible.

Anglo-Chinese potted meat

Serves 6
1lb shin of beef (boneless)
6oz tin Chinese Barbecue Sauce (Hoi-Sin)
4oz margarine
condensed consommé to cover

Cut up the shin and place in a baking dish. Pour over Chinese Barbecue Sauce and bake in the oven with any other dishes till the meat is roasted to a very dark brown (1½ hours at least). Chop the contents of the pan finely in the food processor with the margarine till smooth. Pot. When cold, cover with condensed consommé, and leave overnight. Eat cold with hot toast.

There is a lovely, smug feeling as you think of mortars and pestles and watch your meattie whizzing away. And Ye olde Chinese Take-Away is now as much part of British life as crumpets and the Parish Church.

Bulk for breakfast

Although I often wake with a feeling of anxiety, the thought of breakfast usually cheers me up. In fact I get too cheerful, and I notice friends avoid me in the early hours.

'I wouldn't mind if you were quiet and depressed', one of them said, 'like the rest of us, but with your mindless chatter, and your infernal transistor, and your singing all the wrong notes in all the wrong sort of operas (I sing both Tristan *and* Isolde a.m.) and your conspicuous consumption' – he warmed to his theme – 'and your toast crumbs and your eating marmalade and kippers *at the same time* and yammering away about spirituality with your mouth full . . .'

He paused for breath, and I won't continue, as I feel you have got the point.

I have always been robust about breakfast and have had to be. In my childhood we had it with my grandparents, and it was a hearty repast of black bread, pickled herrings, raw onions (you ate them like an apple) and lemon tea in large glasses without milk but with rum. Perhaps it was the rum which made me cheerful but I was very bright in the morning at school.

My teacher said I had a nice disposition, but in fact after two glasses I was nearly pickled in good old Slav fashion, and even at the age of six smiled benignly and knowingly at everyone.

'A rum sort of kid, that,' said someone. Alas, he spoke wiser than he knew!

It is very pleasant to take breakfast with people who say their prayers before they tuck into their cereals and fried eggs. The devotions seem to settle their anxieties (after all, God must be in them somewhere) and make them more attentive to others. They pass things more. That is why it is so nice to have breakfast with nuns, monks and friars.

I heartily recommend breakfast with the Sisters of Sion at their conference centre at Belinter in Ireland. The food is as delicious as their hospitality, which is saying a lot.

Sister Maura gave me this recipe for home-made Muesli. It is very good and cheaper than the commercial mixes. Try it with prayer!

Sister Maura's muesli

Mix the dry ingredients thoroughly. Mix the oil and honey or molasses (molasses is more nutritious though not sweet enough for some) together. Combine the wet and dry ingredients well, trying to avoid any lumps.

Spread the mixture on deep baking sheets about 1½ inches deep. Bake for about 20 minutes at 300°F Gas 2 150°C, stirring from time to time.

For greater bulk and economy Sister Maura rolls in a packet of All Bran to the cooled mixture.

5 cups raw oats
1 cup sesame seeds
1 cup sunflower seeds
1 cup wheat germ
1 cup desiccated coconut
1 cup soya flour
1 cup vegetable oil
1 cup honey, or molasses, or a combination of honey and molasses
Optional:
½ cup bran
½ cup wholemeal flour
1 cup chopped nuts
1 cup milk powder

GRATUITOUS ADVICE

As a minister of religion I am used to giving gratuitous advice. People encourage clerics to speak out on politics or pop stars to muse on religion. In sermons you can't be answered back and though this makes you freer, it also makes you long-winded. Though one nun I know did get up during a public service and say, 'Father this is not so', or something like that. But she was a lady of rare strength who has now gone to a better place, where she will get whatever reward is considered suitable for integrity.

Here then are some odd bits of advice which have the same coherence of some (not all) of my sermons, and are I hope equally edifying.

A pinch of advice can be added to taste..

HOW to COOK & LIVE.

Science or snobbery ... No seconds

I was at a dinner party, and just as we were about to eat, everybody started talking about dieting, much to the chagrin of our hostess, who had spared neither expense nor calories for our enrichment.

It was curiously like an ecumenical meeting. Everybody started listing the essential points of their beliefs and dogmas. As we all recited our litanies simultaneously it took some time to sort them out. But they had this in common, they were all passionately held, and quite contradictory, at least on first hearing.

One couple were blessed with simple faith. They held to bananas and cream, which (provided you ate nothing else) worked wonders. You could eat, they said, as many as you liked, piling bananas on bananas, all floating on waves of double cream. They were subjected to a ruthless inquisition, and forced to confess, that though easy to prepare, you probably got slim because by the fourth day you could not face the sight of another banana – or even look at the picture of a cow on a margarine packet, added the wife.

Some held to calories, and some swore by carbohydrates. The latter were the most fervent and unyielding because they couldn't explain what a carbohydrate was, and such is always the way when you know something is true, but don't really understand exactly what it is or why.

One couple held quietly to animal fats. They dieted on duckling in butter sauce, followed by champagne cream, but never never touched margarine. You must eat the purest unsalted butter, they cautioned us. But was this science or snobbery? – we gave each other meaningful glances as we considered the matter, coming to our own conclusions. My own contribution to the debate was passed over in contempt and silence, and I later heard through a third party that my hostess swore a terrible oath that she would never invite me again.

The profiteroles and cream were being passed round again, and all I said was, 'Never eat sweets or take a second helping'. The truth makes you free, but it doesn't make you a social success.

Good and better resolutions . . . Kitchen Frauds

I resolve to measure out flour and sugar over the sink or the waste-bin.

I resolve not to spray paint on a door when my dog can push it open. (My dog was black, the paint was white.)

I resolve to shun half-truths and white lies.

I resolve not to say, 'Who cares?' or 'Why me?'

I resolve not to shrug my shoulders.

I resolve not to look through the laundry basket for the least dirty shirt.

I resolve to buy free-range eggs.

I resolve not to forget my soul.

I resolve to give the birds a meal, even if they are just pigeons.

I resolve to remember that there is also a Nazi in me.

I resolve to be honest even if it hurts others and especially me.

I resolve to keep appointments exactly.

I resolve to make marmalade without using a packet of orange jelly to help it along.

I resolve to improve myself and listen to Radio 3 in the kitchen.

I resolve not to waste time in the launderette watching my washing going round and round and round and . . . I shall take a book of theology with me.

I resolve not to pack margarine in the butter dish.

I resolve not to eat a tin of condensed milk when life gets too much for me. (Evaporated has less calories.)

I resolve not to eat cold baked beans with a spoon from the tin. I shall put the tin on a saucer.

I resolve not to say 'It's unfair!'

I resolve not just to yackety-yack when I pray, but to try and listen. Perhaps God can't get a word in edgeways.

I resolve to give up smoking again after I have started smoking again, and when I start yet again, I resolve to resolve to give it up again.

I resolve to put 1 teaspoon of treacle in the dough for Steak and Kidney Pudding to take away the corpse-like pallor.

I resolve to give up bangers and burgers and try the *Nouvelle Cuisine* instead.

I resolve not to call Jam Roly-Poly 'Dead Baby' in front of strangers.

When I ritually fast, I resolve not to swallow some of my toothpaste and gargle.

I resolve not to think I have to earn God's love.

I resolve not to throw away the skins of baked potatoes.

I resolve to be willing to be last in the queue.

I resolve not to call haddock bits 'Jewish scampi'.

I resolve to remember that Dog Chocs are meant for the dog, not for me.

I resolve not to make too many resolutions.

Index

GOOD FOOD FROM FARTHINGHOE
Nicola Cox

An imaginative and reliable collection of recipes for every type of entertaining, all tried and tested at Nicola Cox's cookery school at Farthinghoe, Northampton-shire.

"Cheerful, chatty and relaxed, she makes entertaining sound easy with delicious and original menus"—*The Times*

ISBN 0 575 03843 8

MAGNOLIA STREET
Louis Golding
New Foreword by Rabbi Lionel Blue

The classic novel of Jewish immigrant life inspired by working-class Manchester during the 1920s.

"A most heartwarming book and a lovely read" – Rabbi Blue

ISBN 0 575 03842 X

GOD OF A HUNDRED NAMES
Prayers and meditations from many faiths and cultures
Collected and arranged by Barbara Greene and Victor Gollancz

Reaching across the barriers of time and place, the prayers in this moving and often surprising collection range in author from Elizabeth I to an Arab chieftain, from Socrates to Edith Sitwell. Together they express the deepest needs of the human spirit.

"A book to cling on to when the world seems falling to bits"—Sir John Betjeman

ISBN 0 575 03645 1

TEENAGE ROMANCE
or How to Die of Embarrassment
Delia Ephron, cartoons by Edward Koren

Sage advice and merciless cartoons tell you How to Hide a Pimple, How to go on a Date, How to Worry.

"Reminds you with laser-beam accuracy of everything about your adolescence you were trying to forget. Read it, then join the Foreign Legion."—Keith Waterhouse

ISBN 0 575 03869 1

HOW TO BE A HAPPY CAT
Charles Platt, cartoons by Gray Jolliffe

The first ever self-help guide for cats. Includes profiles of personality types (from Mad Mousers to Timid Tabbies), and advice on How to Dominate Dogs and How to Choose an Owner. Humans ignore this book at their peril.

ISBN 0 575 03902 7